RACHEL LAMBERT

WILD

FORAGE & MAKE

AND

101 SEASONAL DESSERTS

SWEET

HOXTON MINI PRESS

Contents

AUTUMN

WINTER

Why Forage for Dessert?

'The thrill of finding wild ingredients will give way to kitchen alchemy.'

In a digital world, the real and tangible experience of seeking, touching, smelling, collecting and tasting wild food is precious. Whether for a stolen hour or a day, time spent simply gathering what you find in ignored alleys, forgotten gardens, open fields, woodland edges, wastelands or wild hedgerows can feel deliciously indulgent. This book celebrates the overlooked, misunderstood, and even invasive plants, shrubs and trees that are too often discarded as useless weeds when, really, we've simply forgotten their worth. Foraging is both satisfying and rewarding: a simple act that soothes the stresses of life and prompts us to notice what nature freely provides throughout the year.

Back home, the thrill of finding wild ingredients will give way to kitchen alchemy: baking, blending or cooking with sugary infusions. These recipes celebrate my love of sweet things, and the wild diversity of natural and exciting flavours that you could never find in supermarket-bought treats. From the first greens and yellow flowers of spring, to the petals and fresh spices of summer, the fruits and berries of autumn and the roots of winter, this book will introduce you to seasonal desserts like you've never experienced them.

How My Love of Wild Baking Began

There's something about the combination of foraging and sweetness that has always been irresistible to me. I was brought up on home-cooking, sweet baking and wild adventures. My mum was a devoted proponent of sugar; my dad believed in exploring – whether on foot, by bike or by boat. Homemade cordials, cakes or treats were a daily affair, punctuating the day and the end of meals; thus my 'naturally' sweet tooth was shaped.

As a child growing up in the city, our annual blackberry-picking trip was my first taste of the deliciousness to be found in nature. But it wasn't until I was in my 20s, when my friend Martin made a throw-away comment about a plant growing in a wall being edible, that my eyes were suddenly opened to the possibilities of foraging. I started to see both countryside landscapes and urban green spaces as potential places to find wild food. Beginning with simple savoury cook-ups it took me another decade to realise I could combine my love of sweet bakes and foraged ingredients. My first successful experiment was a Nettle and Honey Cake (p.30). It was another pivotal moment.

Foraging has become an integral part of my life because I yearned for something that modern conveniences couldn't provide. I wasn't sure exactly what I was missing, but I loved returning home with pockets of foraged seeds to spice up a slice of pear cake (p.152) or gorse flowers to infuse into cocktails (p.76). There's nothing like the taste of zingy sorrel leaves straight from the spring hedgerow for a green sorrel tart (p.56), or gathering armfuls of autumn rosehips while anticipating making a tangy icing to glaze homemade biscuits (p.212).

Wild and Sweet Flavours

'Foraged ingredients can open up your taste buds.'

As a cook rather than a chef, I delight in uncomplicated puddings that show off wild aromas – either subtly or boldly. Not only do foraged ingredients bring a sense of adventure and colour to the table, they bring a range of forgotten flavours, too. All cultivated ingredients originate from wild foods, yet over thousands of years these plants have been hybridised and modified; in the process, many diverse idiosyncrasies of flavour have been lost. Foraged ingredients can open up your taste buds.

The flavour 'sweet' has a certain allure for many humans, and I am one of them. Yet here you'll find a wide range of interpretations of this common flavour: from fruity to tangy to bitter to aromatic to floral, and many shades in between. I also choose to cook with unrefined sugars, dark sugars, honey and fruit sugars. These add flavour as well as sweetness and retain more natural nutrients, such as calcium, magnesium and iron, than their white counterpart.

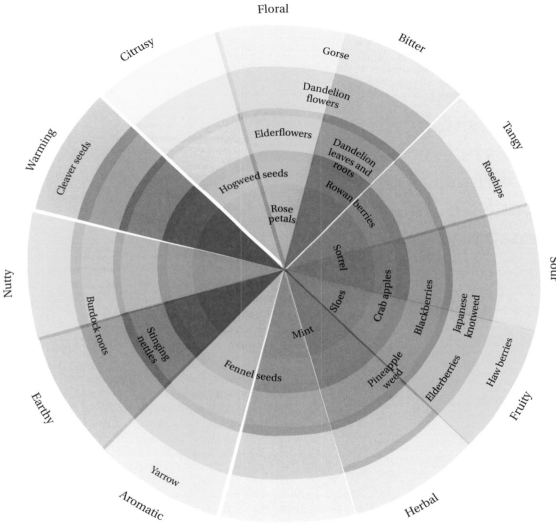

Floral

Citrusy

Bitter

Gorse

Dandelion flowers

Tangy

Warming

Cleaver seeds

Elderflowers

Dandelion leaves and roots

Rosehips

Hogweed seeds

Rowan berries

Rose petals

Sorrel

Sour

Nutty

Burdock roots

Sloes

Crab apples

Blackberries

Japanese knotweed

Haw berries

Stinging nettles

Mint

Earthy

Pineapple weed

Elderberries

Fruity

Fennel seeds

Yarrow

Aromatic

Herbal

Cooling

Mild

Intense

The Yearly Cycle of Foraging

'Every plant, tree or shrub grows to a different, subtle timeframe.'

For ease, this book is laid out according to the seasons, travelling from spring greens through to winter roots. Yet nature doesn't always fit into such neat categories, so please interpret these groupings loosely.

The natural cycle of a plant's life generally starts with the new growth of shoots and leaves, giving way to flowers, which in turn die back so the seeds or fruits can take centre stage, allowing the plant to spread and reseed. As a forager, understanding this rhythm allows an intimate insight into each wild food and its peak picking times – but every plant, tree or shrub grows to a different, subtle timeframe. Sometimes in autumn, depending on the timing and heat of summer, green plant growth can return again, though it is always at its best in spring. Seeds, spices and berries can remain on a plant, shrub or tree for months, or, like elderberries (p.178), appear and fade rather fast. And in the coldest months, when most plants look unimpressive or dead, below the earth roots are conserving energy and storing sugars until the cycle begins again – making this the most nutritious time to dig for them.

There is always an optimum time for each wild food and using sight, touch, smell and taste, along with common sense and the chart opposite, will help you identify it.

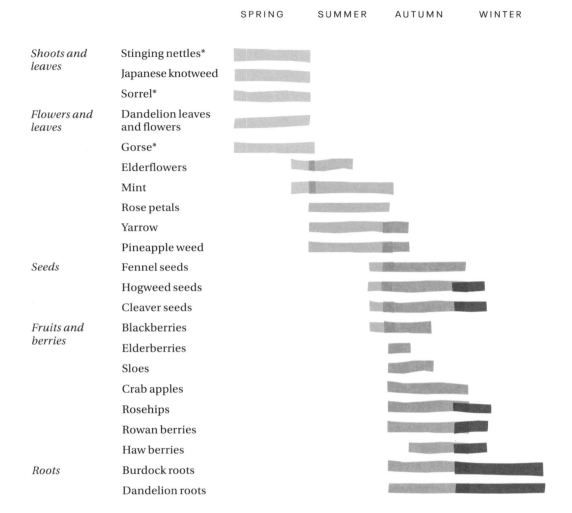

		SPRING	SUMMER	AUTUMN	WINTER

Shoots and leaves
Stinging nettles*
Japanese knotweed
Sorrel*

Flowers and leaves
Dandelion leaves and flowers
Gorse*
Elderflowers
Mint
Rose petals
Yarrow
Pineapple weed

Seeds
Fennel seeds
Hogweed seeds
Cleaver seeds

Fruits and berries
Blackberries
Elderberries
Sloes
Crab apples
Rosehips
Rowan berries
Haw berries

Roots
Burdock roots
Dandelion roots

This seasonal chart shows how a plant's natural life cycle can be roughly mapped against the seasons, helping foragers to pick at the ideal time of year.

* Though stinging nettles, sorrel and gorse are at their most tender (and therefore most delicious) in spring, nettles and sorrel both have a second flush in autumn and gorse flowers grow year round.

Foraging with Care

Foraging can connect you to the bigger picture of how nature fluxes and flourishes. Many plants thrive with being harvested – they are built to be interacted with and fed on by humans, insects, animals, birds and multiple micro-organisms. This perception of a shared world is often counterintuitive to the individualistic culture we live in, yet awareness of our interconnectedness is of immense value.

Worldwide research shows that a connection to people and place has a significant impact on health, wellbeing and happiness; as does eating natural foods. Foraging has the ability to bring us together and feed our bodies, minds and souls. Discovering wild foods transforms an unruly blanket of weeds into a garden of wild ingredients; an overgrown tree laden with fruits into a bottle of vitamin C-rich syrup. This appreciation of commonplace plants can be hugely lacking in our lives, and can offer an essential alternative to the throw-away culture we reside in.

As our wild areas shrink, and diversity declines, it is also key to take a step back and assess our role as foragers. In the UK, weeds like stinging nettles (p.26), Japanese knotweed (p.40) and blackberry-laden brambles (p.166) can take over certain areas and it can be beneficial to ruthlessly harvest them. I have knocked on numerous doors over the years to ask if I can pick unwanted plants from someone else's garden. I rarely come away empty-handed from these requests, and both parties often feel enriched from the exchange (especially if I offer to return with a slice of wild dessert as a thank you). In every area there will be some plants in abundance and others sparsely available, so it's important to be aware of when to pick less or perhaps not at all. Sometimes it feels good to just walk away with empty hands and the satisfaction of having taken care. There are many other abundant weeds just longing for attention, eager to be eaten and rediscovered as glorious ingredients for sweet treats.

Foraging with caution

Accurate identification is key when foraging for wild plants: seeking out an experienced foraging guide in your area can help put your mind and stomach at ease. A few of the plants in this book have some look-alikes that are inedible, tasteless, toxic or even deadly. If you're unsure whether you've found the right plant, don't pick it. Learning about foraging is a journey that takes time and skill and it's best to be cautious and accurate rather than blasé and wrong.

Plus, eating too much of any one food – especially if it's new to you – is never a great idea (I still remember the ill effects of eating too many blackberries as a child!). This book includes important key identifying features (do use these to help you identify, along with the photos) as well as the plants' main and known cautions, offered as a guide only.

Finally, remember to check the laws and rights in your area and country regarding foraging and access to land. In the UK, for example, you must always seek the landowner's permission if you are uprooting a plant.

Here are some questions I always ask myself when foraging:

On what I'm foraging...

- Am I 100% sure I've identified the plant correctly?
- What wild foods are common and thriving in my area?
- Which plants are rare or only just cultivated and need to be left to grow?
- Has it been sprayed or treated with pesticides?
- Can I offer to get rid of an invasive plant and use it as a wild food?
- Do I have to be careful not to aid the spreading of this plant?

On how much I'm foraging...

- Is there enough to pick 30% of leaves, shoots or berries and leave 70% growing?
- If picking flowers or seeds, can I gather just 10% and still leave enough?
- Is the plant invasive and therefore could it be beneficial to pick all or a lot of it?
- Can I take little enough that it's unnoticeable I have picked from here?
- Is there more elsewhere so I don't overpick from one spot?
- Who else might forage here (humans, mammals, birds, insects): have I left enough for them?

On where I'm foraging...

- Can (and should) I plant this wild food via seeds or cuttings to help it become more abundant?
- What conditions does it favour to grow in if I want to help it spread?
- Can I create a wild area in my garden, a window box or in a local community space?
- Who should I ask about picking this wild food: do I need permission from a landowner?
- Can I offer to 'weed' a friend or neighbour's garden to gather the wild foods I want?

Useful Equipment

Besides the usual baking equipment, here are some choice utensils that will make this adventure easier for you, both when you're out foraging and back in the kitchen:

Bag or basket

Resuable cloth bags, recycled plastic bags, baskets or Tupperware containers are all useful for gathering your bounty while out foraging (though I often return home with pockets full of unexpected wild finds, too).

Pen knife or scissors

To make cutting hardy stems easier.

Small trowel, spade and large gardening fork

For digging up roots. A trowel will suffice for dandelion roots (p.252), but you'll need a spade and fork for large burdock roots (p.242).

Thick gloves

For picking stinging nettles (p.26) and spiky plants.

Muslin cloths, nylon cloths or jelly bags

For straining syrups, purées and creams. Make sure the piece of fabric is large enough to stop leakage and use an elastic band to secure it. A fine sieve will also often do the job.

Jam thermometer

Getting the correct setting point is important for jams and preserves, as well as sweets such as Elderberry and Apple Fruit Pastilles (p.182) and Haw Delight (p.234).

Grinder or pestle and mortar

For grinding seeds and making powdered sugars. A manual or electric seed or coffee grinder works well for preparing all of the seeds and sugars in this book. A pestle and mortar will suffice for some, such as fennel seeds (p.134) and dandelion flower sugar (p.67), but not all.

Blender or food processor

I find a simple stick blender is adequate for all of the recipes that require blending here, but you can use a stand blender or food processor if you have one.

Jars and bottles

I sterilise and reuse old jam jars and bottles and have a selection of reusable containers for jams, syrups and cordials. They should have lids and be completely sealable to store wild recipes.

How to Use This Book

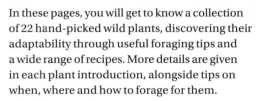

'I'm hoping these pages ignite an irresistible urge to get outdoors and explore your local patch.'

In these pages, you will get to know a collection of 22 hand-picked wild plants, discovering their adaptability through useful foraging tips and a wide range of recipes. More details are given in each plant introduction, alongside tips on when, where and how to forage for them.

The recipes have been created to suit different dietary needs, dessert preferences and sweet cravings. Some recipes require fresh ingredients, while others incorporate dried seeds, leaves or flowers so they can be baked and enjoyed out of season, too. Many have components that can be pre-made, such as Japanese Knotweed Jam (p.45) or Elderflower Cordial (p.90), both of which are great to keep in the fridge until required. Numerous berries and fruits benefit from some time in the freezer, too, to preserve and keep till needed. I recommend reading recipes through thoroughly before embarking on your wild and sweet cooking, as some require a little planning.

I've chosen these plants for their broad availability across Europe, North America and Australasia and their ability to thrive in both rural and urban settings (though no plant can be available everywhere). Whether an overgrown area of your garden, a forgotten path, a field or a vast new vista to explore, I'm hoping these pages ignite an irresistible urge to get outdoors and explore your local patch. And I hope, too, that this book becomes a lifelong companion for you. Here, you can return to the same plants for years to come, discovering different sides to their dessert potential through the seasons. May they give you as much pleasure as they do me.

Above: Foraging for mint (p.94). Right: Mint and Coconut Fridge Cake (p.98).

Left: Yarrow (p.114), mint (p.94) and pineapple weed (p.124). Above: Foraging for sorrel (p.50).

Left: Collecting crab apples (p.198). Above: Rowan Marmalade Pudding (p.228).

Spring

There's a buzz in the air,
the ground feels different, the
scenery has changed colour
and there's plenty to forage.
This season is all about
greens and as the sap rises,
so do the nutrition and the
sweetness in the leaves
and stems. Crisp mornings
still urge a patience though:
a moment to reflect on
the season awakening and
to notice the first of the
yellow flowers, as attractive
to bees and other pollinators
as they are to a forager.

Stinging Nettles

Urtica dioica (Urticaceae)

There is a day each year when the fresh scent of nettles in the air tells me spring has truly arrived. It was my friend's son, Arthur, and his seven-year-old classmates who first told me nettles taste sweet when I taught them how to cautiously eat one raw. Their young taste buds inspired me to create more desserts from these maligned plants. Sometimes they're described as tasting like spinach, yet nettles are hard to compare to any other green with their deep, earthy flavour and coarse, vibrant leaves.

It is all too easy to disregard common nettles as a useless weed but they have extraordinary qualities. They are nourishing and revitalising – containing up to 20% protein, as well as iron, vitamins C, B, E and K and beta-carotene, and are a good overall tonic for the body. They improve circulation and lower blood sugar, can treat anaemia, and provide an energy boost. They are also abundant, thrive well when their tops are snipped off and cooking them completely removes the sting. Stinging nettles are native to Europe, Asia and the Middle East and have been introduced to some parts of North and South America and Southern Africa.

Main identifying features

Nettles grow up to 1½m/5ft tall with hairy stems. Leaves grow opposite each other and have pointed tips and deeply toothed edges. Flowers are greenish, sometimes purple-tinged, and tendril like.

When to forage

The leaves are at their best throughout spring (stop picking when tendril-like flowers emerge in late spring), but do have a second flush in autumn.

Where to forage

Road verges, woods, hedgerows, cultivated ground and river banks; in fact almost anywhere nettles can grow, they do. Woods and shadier areas help keep them sweeter and more tender for longer.

How to forage

Protect bare skin, wear a thick pair of gardening gloves (or similar) and cut off the top 4–6 leaves with scissors.

Cautions

The tiny hairs covering nettles contain formic acid and will sting, causing a red rash and slight swelling that normally settles down after a few hours or days.

Other notable varieties

Small nettle (*Urtica urens*)

Nettles are most tender (and delicious) in spring: snip off the top cluster of leaves from each plant.

Nettle and Honey Cake

Serves 12

When I first mentioned this cake on a foraging course, otherwise curious children were revolted by the idea. When I produced it at the end of the walk, they were grabbing for it before I'd finished cutting it and not one piece was left. It's also utterly delicious drizzled with Gorse Flower Syrup (p.73).

Ingredients

100g/3½oz nettle tops

250g/9oz clear honey

100g/3½oz dark muscovado sugar

225g/8oz butter

3 large free-range eggs, beaten

300g/10oz self-raising flour (or 300g/10oz plain flour plus 4 tsp baking powder), sifted

Method

Preheat the oven to 150°C/130°C fan/300°F and line a 20cm/8in square or round cake tin with baking parchment.

Place the nettle tops in a steamer basket over a saucepan of simmering water and steam for 5 minutes, then set aside to cool. Place the honey, sugar and butter in a small saucepan over a low heat and stir until melted and combined, then take off the heat.

Once the nettles are cooled, add them to a food processor with the eggs (or use a stick blender) and blitz to a smooth, green pulp. Add the flour to a large bowl and gradually beat in the melted sugar and butter mix. It will be a lovely toffee colour. Pour in the puréed nettle and egg mix and beat together until combined into a wonderful green cake mixture.

Pour into the cake tin and bake for 1 hour, or until a skewer inserted into the centre comes out clean or the cake springs back when gently touched in the centre. Allow to cool for a few minutes before removing from the tin onto a cooling rack. This cake will keep in an airtight container for up to 5 days, and also freezes well.

Nettle and Fennel Syrup

Makes approx. 750ml/1⅓ pints
Vegan and gluten-free

I often dilute this dark, rich nettle syrup to make a sweet drink, which always disappears surprisingly quickly on foraging walks. The inclusion of fennel lifts the syrup out of the darkness a little. It's also delicious in Nettle Baklava (p.34) or Nutty Nettle Energy Balls (p.37).

Ingredients

3 tbsp fennel seeds, freshly ground or crushed

200g/7oz nettle tops

approx. 500–800g/1lb 2oz–1lb 12oz soft brown or demerara sugar

1–3 tbsp lemon juice (if not using immediately)

Method

Put the fennel seeds, nettle tops and 800ml/ 1½ pints water in a large saucepan, bring to the boil then cover and simmer for 40 minutes. Take off the heat and strain through a fine sieve or muslin cloth, using a wooden spoon to help squeeze all the liquid out.

Measure the liquid, and for every 1 millilitre add 1 gram of sugar – for example, 500g/1lb 2oz sugar for 500ml/18fl oz liquid. Place the nettle liquid and sugar back in the saucepan and heat, uncovered, to a very gentle simmer, then reduce the heat until just steaming and cook for 30 minutes, stirring occasionally.

If using the syrup immediately, ladle out the amount you need. For the rest, add 1 tablespoon of lemon juice for every 250ml/8½fl oz liquid, allow to cool, then decant into sterilised bottles and seal. The syrup will keep well in the fridge for up to 6 months.

Nettle Powder

Makes 25g/1oz | Vegan and gluten-free

This is a convenient way to process and store nettles for nettle energy balls (p.36 and p.37), enabling you to access their spring nutrition throughout the year. I also sometimes blend it with icing sugar to make either an alternative dusting for doughnuts or to dip glass rims in to serve drinks using wild cordials.

Ingredients

125g/4½oz nettle tops

Method

First, wash the nettles tops and dry them as much as possible: either in a salad spinner or between tea towels.

Now to fully dry them – there are several ways to do this. For one, you can use a dehydrator, if you have one, following the manufacturer's instructions. If you don't, and you're baking anyway, the easiest way is to place the nettles on a large baking tray and, once you've finished using the oven, turn it off, place the tray on the bottom shelf and leave for 2 hours or longer. Depending how efficient your oven is at retaining heat, this could be enough to dry out the nettles. Alternatively, place the nettles on a baking tray and pop in the oven at the lowest temperature for a couple of hours or until dried.

Or, if you've plenty of time and space, you could lay the nettles out on a large baking tray, or on clean tea towels or cooling racks. Leave in a warm space to air-dry for 48 hours, or until dry. Do turn them intermittently to check and separate any clumps of wet nettles.

To make the nettle powder, the leaves need to be dry enough that they crumble easily when touched or rubbed. Before they are powdered they can still sting a little, so use gloves to transfer them to a pestle and mortar, spice grinder or clean coffee grinder, then grind to a powder. Store in a sterilised jar in a cool, dark place; the powder will keep well for up to 6 months.

Nettle Baklava

Serves 8–10 | Vegan

Sticky and sweet, the Nettle and Fennel Syrup (p.32) gives this baklava a whole new level of goodness. One spring birthday, I carried a full container of it on a five-mile walk through pounding winds for my weather-hardy friends. We devoured the whole lot on the way.

Ingredients

8 sheets of filo pastry, cut in half

75ml/2½fl oz sunflower oil (or 75g/2¾oz butter, melted), plus extra for greasing

200g/7oz walnuts, finely chopped

250ml/8½fl oz Nettle and Fennel Syrup (p.32), chilled

Method

Preheat the oven to 180°C/160°C fan/350°F and grease a 20x30cm/8x12in baking tin.

Trim the filo pastry sheets to fit inside the baking tin, then lay 1 sheet of filo in the tin, brush with oil or melted butter and layer on a second, continuing until 5 oiled sheets of filo are laid down. Evenly spread half the chopped walnuts over the surface of the filo, then layer another 5 sheets of filo on top, brushing each one with oil or butter as you layer.

Sprinkle over the remaining chopped walnuts (setting aside a few for decoration) and the remaining filo sheets, brushing each with oil or butter as you layer. With a sharp knife, score into strips lengthways, then score diagonally to create diamond shapes.

Decorate with the reserved nuts then bake in the oven for 45 minutes, or until golden, being careful not to let it burn. Remove from the oven and immediately spoon over the cold syrup; it will sizzle as it absorbs the liquid. Leave for at least 2 hours before cutting along the scored lines and serving. The baklava will keep, stored in an airtight container at room temperature, for up to 3 days.

Lemon and Nettle Energy Balls

Makes 12–15 | Vegan and gluten-free

These zingy energy balls are easy to make and rather addictive! Once you've made your Nettle Powder (p.33), they can be made any time of year. (Recipe pictured on pp.36–37.)

Ingredients

250g/9oz pitted dates

3 tbsp lemon juice

60g/2¼oz cashew nuts

2 tbsp Nettle Powder (p.33)

For the coating

3 tbsp sesame seeds, desiccated coconut or Nettle Powder (p.33)

Method

If you have a food processor, simply add all the ingredients and blitz to a smooth mixture.

If making by hand, finely chop the dates and place in a small bowl, then cover with the lemon juice and set aside for 5 minutes. Meanwhile, finely grind the cashew nuts in a seed grinder, or place in a strong, sealable plastic bag and finely crush with a rolling pin (or crush patiently in a pestle and mortar). Add to the date mixture, along with the nettle powder, and combine thoroughly with a spoon or your fingertips until the mixture is smooth and somewhat sticky and can be rolled into balls.

Shape the mixture into 12–15 balls, each about 5cm/2in across. Pour your chosen coating into a separate shallow bowl (or use all three coatings, divided into three separate bowls, for a variety of flavours) and roll the balls in it until evenly coated. Store in an airtight container in the fridge and use within 1 week; they're best eaten at room temperature.

Nutty Nettle Energy Balls

Makes 12–15 | Vegan and gluten-free

There are a thousand ways to make energy balls, each with different qualities to enjoy. These are sweetened with Nettle and Fennel Syrup (p.32) and have a powdered nettle sugar coating that gives them a delicious, almost seaweed-like flavour. (Recipe pictured on pp.36–37.)

Ingredients

185g/6¾oz pitted dates

3 tbsp Nettle and Fennel Syrup (p.32)

90g/3¼oz ground or finely chopped nuts of your choice

3 tbsp Nettle Powder (p.33)

2 tbsp unrefined icing sugar

Method

If you have a food processor, tip in the dates, syrup, nuts and half the nettle powder and blitz to a smooth mixture. Set aside for 10 minutes, so the syrup can infuse into the mixture, before rolling into smooth balls.

If making by hand, finely chop the dates and place in a small bowl, then cover with the nettle and fennel syrup and set aside for 10 minutes. Then add the nuts and half the nettle powder, and combine thoroughly with a spoon or your fingertips until the mixture is smooth and can be rolled into balls.

Shape the mixture into 12–15 balls, each about 5cm/2in across.

For the coating, combine the icing sugar and remaining nettle powder in a shallow bowl and roll the balls until coated. Store in an airtight container in the fridge, sprinkled with any leftover coating, and use within 1 week; they're best eaten at room temperature.

An assortment of Lemon and Nettle Energy Balls (p.36) and Nutty Nettle Energy Balls (p.37).

Japanese Knotweed

Reynoutria japonica (Polygonaceae)

There is a particular, satisfying popping sound made by snapping a hollow stem of Japanese knotweed, followed by a splutter as the sap escapes. This oft-dreaded plant can grow in the blink of an eye – pushing through concrete and damaging buildings – yet it is so utterly delicious. I think of it fondly by its other name, 'donkey rhubarb', as its flavour is indeed reminiscent of rhubarb, though not quite as sharp and a little fruitier.

It's native to Japan, Southeast China, Korea and Taiwan, where it's revered for its health-giving qualities. It is both a stunning and an alien-looking plant in the landscapes of Europe and North America, where it has now been introduced. High in vitamins C and A and antioxidants, knotweed can boost immunity and assist cardiovascular health. Despite friends' caution at eating this plant, it is always received well in cakes or syrupy toppings.

Main identifying features

Grows up to 3m/10ft tall. Pale green to dusty pink in colour with shades of mottled red and purple, and asparagus-like tips. Leggy, hollow stems punctuated with notches.

When to forage

The shoots start to grow in early spring and can grow up to 30cm/1ft a day. By late spring to early summer, they can become too fibrous to use.

Where to forage

Roadsides, damp areas (the banks of streams and rivers), the outskirts of urban areas and wastelands.

How to forage

Cut the shoots with a knife (the best shoots are up to 60cm/2ft tall) and carefully bag up the pieces, ensuring that no cut fragments are left behind.

Cautions

In many countries it is illegal to aid the spread of Japanese knotweed, so be very careful not to drop any parts (even small pieces) when cutting and harvesting. Cooking discarded parts before you get rid of them also ensures they cannot spread. The plant's undesirability means it is often treated with pesticides; exercise caution and do not pick in areas where this might be the case, especially urban areas. You should always look out for signs labelling treated areas.

Japanese Knotweed Frangipane

Makes 9 squares

Lovely, tart tones mingled with a soft, almondy topping, a thick, jammy centre and a sweet, crunchy base: what more could you want in a dessert? Eat on its own or with crème fraîche.

For the base

120g/4¼oz butter, softened

200g/7oz wholemeal (wheat, spelt or rye) flour

50g/2oz soft brown sugar

40g/1½oz ground almonds

For the topping

100g/3½oz soft brown sugar

125g/4½oz butter, softened

150g/5oz ground almonds

1 large free-range egg

125g/4½oz Japanese Knotweed Jam (p.45)

150g/5oz prepared Japanese knotweed (peeled and leaves, tops and papery notches removed – see Tip), cut into 1–2cm/½–¾in slices

Method

Preheat the oven to 180°C/160°C fan/350°F and line a 20cm/8in square tin with baking parchment.

In a large bowl, combine all the ingredients for the base to create a smooth batter, then scoop into the tin and press down to make an even surface. Bake for 10 minutes, then take out of the oven and leave to cool.

Meanwhile, combine the sugar, butter, ground almonds and egg for the topping. When the base is cooled, evenly coat with the jam, then scatter half of the Japanese knotweed slices over the top. Dot the mixture evenly across the jam and knotweed; this will spread when cooking so don't worry too much about covering all of it. Sprinkle the remaining knotweed slices on top, pressing them down slightly, and bake for 30 minutes or until the top is firm and browned around the edges.

Leave to cool in the tin, then cut into 9 squares. These will keep, refrigerated, for up to 4 days.

Tip

The base of Japanese knotweed and the outer layers of older stems can be quite fibrous and are best discarded. On younger stems, peel where needed, but most of the outer parts will soften well with cooking and don't need to be removed.

Japanese Knotweed Purée

Makes 500g/1lb 2oz | Vegan and gluten-free

An unembellished, unsweetened ingredient for cake, jam and all the recipes in this section. It is also an essential ingredient in Elderflower and Knotweed Fool (p.86). The leftover liquid is perfect for making the Japanese Knotweed Syrup recipe opposite.

Ingredients

1kg/2lb 3oz prepared Japanese knotweed (peeled and leaves, tops and papery notches removed – see Tip on p.42), cut into 1–2cm/ ½–¾in slices

Method

Place the knotweed slices and 375ml/13fl oz water in a large saucepan over a medium heat. Bring to the boil, then turn down the heat, cover with a lid and simmer for 15 minutes or until soft and mushy.

Mash the pulp a little and, if you're confident it doesn't contain hard, fibrous parts, you can use the purée as it is. If not, press through a colander or large-holed sieve into a large bowl and discard the fibrous pulp left in the colander.

Place the smooth pulp in a jelly bag or muslin cloth over a bowl and allow the liquid to drip through for 1 hour. Put the liquid aside for making syrup (see recipe opposite) and the purée is ready to use. If not using immediately, store in the fridge in an airtight container for up to 4 days, or freeze (I'd suggest dividing and freezing in portions) for up to 6 months.

Japanese Knotweed Jam

Makes 400g/14oz | Vegan and gluten-free

A delectably thick, fruity-flavoured jam that is gorgeous as a layer in Japanese Knotweed Frangipane (p.42) or smothered on to toast.

Ingredients

300g/10oz Japanese Knotweed Purée (see opposite page)

300g/10oz soft brown sugar

Method

Place both the purée and sugar in a small pan over a medium heat and bring to the boil while stirring. Allow to bubble for 15 minutes or until it reaches 95°C/200°F on a sugar thermometer, checking that it doesn't burn.

I find the mixture spits a lot, so use a splatter guard or part-cover with a lid to stop it getting everywhere. It's ready when it is dark in colour and drops heavily off the spoon like a thick fruit spread. Store in a sterilised jar in the fridge for up to 6 months.

Japanese Knotweed Syrup

Makes 750ml/1⅓ pints
Vegan and gluten-free

This irresistible syrup combines sweetness with a pleasant, lingering sourness, and has been a welcome addition to my collection of wild syrups to dilute for drinks. Use it in Japanese Knotweed Filo Cake (p.48) or drizzled over Japanese Knotweed Fruit and Nut Cake (p.47).

Ingredients

500ml/18fl oz knotweed water (reserved from making the Japanese Knotweed Purée opposite)

500g/1lb 2oz golden caster sugar

Method

Place the knotweed liquid and sugar in a medium saucepan over a medium heat. Stir until the sugar dissolves then bring to the boil and leave to simmer for 10–15 minutes to thicken and reduce the liquid. Store in a sterilised bottle in the fridge for up to 6 months.

Tip

If you haven't made Knotweed Purée, you can prepare knotweed water by simmering 500g/1lb 2oz Japanese knotweed in 375ml/13fl oz water for 10 minutes. Pass through a sieve or colander, reserving the liquid, then discard the knotweed.

Japanese Knotweed Fruit and Nut Cake

Serves 8–12 | Vegan

Given how easy to make and low fat this moist cake is, it's really surprisingly good. The alchemy of fruit, nuts, wholemeal flour and Japanese knotweed unexpectedly creates an aroma of chocolate, and I like to make my slice a little more decadent by drizzling it with Japanese Knotweed Syrup (p.45) or cream.

Ingredients

100g/3½oz plain flour

125g/4½oz wholemeal flour

2 tsp bicarbonate of soda

200g/7oz soft brown sugar

50g/2oz roughly chopped almonds or hazelnuts

50g/2oz chopped dates

300g/10oz Japanese Knotweed Purée (p.44)

50ml/1¾fl oz vegetable oil

Method

Preheat the oven to 180°C/160°C fan/350°F and line a 20cm/8in cake tin with baking parchment.

In a large mixing bowl, combine the dry ingredients, then stir in the knotweed purée and oil and combine well. Pour into the cake tin and bake for 1 hour or until a skewer inserted into the centre comes out clean. Allow to cool in the tin for 30 minutes, then transfer to a cooling rack and leave to cool completely before slicing. Store in an airtight container at room temperature, and eat within 5 days.

Japanese Knotweed Filo Cake

Serves 12

This sticky, dense dessert is based on a *portokalopita* cake – a Greek dessert made with filo and yoghurt and soaked in syrup. My wild version is lusciously moist and infused with the citrussy flavour of Japanese Knotweed Syrup (p.45).

Ingredients

300g/10oz filo pastry

120ml/4fl oz sunflower or (non-virgin) olive oil

3 free-range eggs

100g/3½oz Japanese Knotweed Purée (p.44)

150g/5oz full-fat yoghurt

100g/3½oz golden granulated sugar

1½ tsp baking powder

300ml/10fl oz Japanese Knotweed Syrup (p.45), plus extra for serving

Method

First prepare the filo by individually scrunching up each sheet and leaving them to air-dry for a few hours or, better still, place the scrunched sheets on a baking tray at the lowest temperature in the oven for 1 hour. After this you should be able to crumble the pastry into small flakes, making sure no moist clumps remain.

Preheat the oven to 180°C/160°C fan/350°F and grease a 20cm/8in square baking tin.

Combine the oil, eggs, knotweed purée, yoghurt, sugar and baking powder in a bowl, then blitz with a stick blender, tip into a stand blender or whisk thoroughly by hand. Scatter a handful of the filo pastry flakes into the baking tin and pour over the yoghurt mixture. Stir together, making sure all the filo is coated in the yoghurt mixture, then continue adding the filo pastry to the tin and stirring until it's all absorbed.

Bake in the oven for 35–40 minutes, until golden on top. As soon as the cake is out of the oven, prick the top all over with a skewer or fork and pour over the syrup. It will look like too much, but just let it soak in for at least an hour. Cut and serve, drizzled with extra syrup. If not eating immediately, this cake will keep in the fridge for up to 5 days.

Sorrel

Rumex acetosa (Polygonaceae)

Sharp and tangy, there's always someone on every foraging course I lead that falls in love with sorrel. Like lemons, it has a fabulous sourness that makes me wince and screw my face up if eaten raw. Still, I can't resist the zestiness it brings to desserts – and it's an excellent source of vitamins A and C and potassium. It's the oxalic acid in the plant (also found in plants such as rhubarb, Japanese knotweed, p.40, and blackberries, p.166) that provides its distinctive kick. Common sorrel (*Rumex acetosa*) is native to Europe, much of Asia and the Middle East and has been introduced in areas of North and South America.

Though the larger leaves of common sorrel (pictured in the bottom half of the image opposite) are the most convenient to cook with, they're not the only variety I forage for. Carpets of green weeds are transformed into ingredients when you start to spot the distinctive leaves of various sorrels. In forests and other shady areas, I often spot wood sorrel (*Oxalis acetosella*) whose pretty leaves (pictured top left) are perfect for edible decorations. The delicate leaves of sheep's sorrel (*Rumex acetosella* – the sharpest-tasting variety, pictured middle right) can be found in more urban areas, including wastelands, walls and grassy lawns, as well as in rural fields, hedgerows and any other places there is acid soil.

Main identifying features

Grows up to 60cm/2ft tall. Channelled stems and arrow-shaped, delicate leaves with tails growing either side of the stem that come to an absolute point (pictured in the bottom half of the image opposite). Flowers are green, pink or red discs on slender spikes.

When to forage

Throughout spring, though a second flush can appear in autumn after the plant has flowered in summer.

Where to forage

Fields and hedgerows, gardens, parks and grassy areas.

How to forage

Pick the leaves before the flowers appear.

Cautions

Sorrel contains oxalic acid, which isn't good in large amounts and can aggravate rheumatism, arthritis, gout, kidney stones and hyperacidity.

Other notable varieties

Sheep's sorrel (*Rumex acetosa*)
Wood sorrel (*Oxalis acetosella*)
Mountain sorrel (*Oxyria digyna*)

Wood sorrel (above) makes an excellent edible decoration, while common sorrel (right) is best for making desserts.

Sorrel Ice Cream

Makes 1 litre/1¾ pints | Gluten-free

A delightful no-churn, light and fluffy ice cream recipe, oozing with the flavour of fresh sorrel. When the mood for decadence grabs me, I like to serve this with slightly warmed Nettle Baklava (p.34) and enjoy the sensation of the cold, tart ice cream melting against the warm, sweet baklava.

Ingredients

4 free-range eggs, separated

85g/3oz golden caster sugar

75g/2¾oz sorrel leaves, washed

300ml/10fl oz double cream

wood sorrel leaves, to decorate (optional)

Method

In a large, spotlessly clean bowl, whisk the egg whites until they form stiff peaks. Slowly pour in the caster sugar as you continue to whisk the mixture, whisking until the egg whites are glossy and stiff.

Put the sorrel leaves and cream in a blender and blend until completely smooth, then pour the mixture into a bowl and whisk until the mixture forms soft peaks. Whisk in the egg yolks before folding the mixture into the egg whites. Gently stir until thoroughly blended.

Pour into a 1½-litre/2¾-pint lidded, freezer-proof container and freeze for a minimum of 2 hours, or preferably overnight (though it will keep, in the freezer, for up to 5 months). Serve in scoops, decorated with wood sorrel leaves, if available.

Sorrel Tart

Serves 12

Whenever I find fresh sorrel leaves, I envision devouring this rich, tangy tart. According to my friend Tue, this is what the colour green should taste like – and it's perfect served just as it is.

For the pastry

75g/2¾oz cold, salted butter, cubed

100g/3½oz plain flour, sifted

50g/2oz wholemeal flour, sifted

1 tbsp dark brown sugar

free-range egg white, beaten, for brushing

For the filling

200g/7oz sorrel leaves and stems, washed

1 free-range egg

4 free-range egg yolks

100g/3½oz golden granulated sugar

150ml/5fl oz double cream

Method

To make the pastry, add the butter to a bowl, then add the flours and sugar and rub between your fingertips until the mixture is well combined and resembles breadcrumbs. Add 1 tablespoon of water to bind the pastry together, adding a tiny bit more water if needed. Wrap the dough in baking parchment or waxed paper and refrigerate for 30 minutes.

Preheat the oven to 190°C/170°C fan/375°F and grease a 20cm/8in flan tin.

Roll out the pastry into a rough circle just larger than the diameter of the flan tin (around 25cm/10in across), then place in the tin, pressing it gently into the sides, and cut off any overhanging pastry. Prick the base all over with a fork, place a piece of baking parchment larger than the tin on top, then fill with baking beans or uncooked rice and bake for 25 minutes. Remove the baking parchment and beans or rice, brush lightly with enough egg white to seal any holes and bake for another 5 minutes, or until golden. Remove from the oven and reduce the oven temperature to 170°C/150°C fan/325°F.

Meanwhile, place the sorrel in a blender and blitz until smooth, then gently squeeze through a jelly bag or muslin cloth to extract all the juice. There should be about 150ml/5fl oz juice. If you have less, squeeze the pulp some more to see if you can make up the amount, or add a little water.

Next, in a large bowl, whisk together the egg, egg yolks and sugar. Add the cream, followed by the sorrel juice, and mix until it is a uniform pale green colour. Pour or ladle into the pastry base and, very carefully and slowly, place in the oven. Bake for 35 minutes, or until the filling is set in the middle. Allow to cool before slicing and serving. The tart will keep in the fridge for up to 5 days.

Sorrel Granita

Serves 4 | Vegan and gluten-free

Sorrel is refreshing. Sorrel blended with crushed, sweetened ice is even more so. This granita is simple to make and the emerald colour seems to heighten the sharp green flavour of the leaves.

Ingredients

100g/3½oz sorrel leaves, washed

50g/2oz golden granulated sugar

Method

Put the sorrel leaves and 300ml/10fl oz water in a blender and blend until smooth, then add the sugar and blend again. Strain through a jelly bag or muslin cloth and squeeze every last drop into a 500ml/18fl oz lidded, freezer-proof container.

Freeze for 2 hours, then remove from the freezer and mash the edges of the granita with a fork. Freeze for a further 1 hour, then repeat mashing the edges. Return to the freezer for 12 hours or until frozen completely (it will keep in the freezer for up to 3 months).

To serve, mash the granita completely with a fork, then serve it in glasses or small bowls.

Dandelion Leaves and Flowers

Taraxacum officinale (Asteraceae)

Dandelions are strong in more ways than one; they are robust, grow ubiquitously and the leaves have a zealous, bitter bite to them. Yet their sun-yellow petals are more delicate in flavour – light and floral with just a tinge of bitter – and their invaluable nutrition is often overlooked. To children, I introduce them as the A, B, C, E plant (naming their vitamins) or the lion's tooth plant (*dent-de-lion*) in reflection of their toothed leaf shape. I don't mention their iron, magnesium, potassium and calcium content, though I know they'll benefit from it anyway.

Native to Europe and Asia as well as certain areas of North and South America, North Africa and Australasia, they have now been introduced widely across the world. These common plants have a reputation for being a diuretic, hence their French name: *pissenlit*. However, dandelions are actually a very mild diuretic and any potential nutritional loss is countered by their high mineral content, particularly in regards to potassium. Even their bitterness is of value, signifying the dandelion's natural detoxifying abilities and acting as an essential partner to create that well-loved flavour: bittersweet. But don't just make use of what's above the ground; in winter, dandelion roots (p.252) can be unearthed and roasted to create warming, comforting desserts.

Main identifying features

Grows up to 35cm/1ft tall with hollow, branchless stems filled with a milky sap. Leaves are deeply toothed and grow from the base of the plant. Yellow flowers transform into white, fluffy 'clocks' when turning to seed.

When to forage

The leaves grow throughout the year, though are best in spring. Flowers appear and are most profuse in late spring, though can continue through to autumn.

Where to forage

Dandelions are extremely easily found in sunny areas, gardens, growing up between pavements, in parks, grassy fields and road verges.

How to forage

Pick the leaves and yellow flowers; flowers close overnight but open again each morning (unless they've started to go to seed).

Dandelion Petal Syrup

Makes 200ml/6¾fl oz | Vegan and gluten-free

Surprisingly nutty with an underlying hint of dandelion petals, I drizzle this syrup over Dandelion Griddle Cakes (p.68) for a sugary, detoxifying treat or dilute it for children's drinks.

Ingredients

150 dandelion flowers, petals picked

175ml/6fl oz boiling water

approx. 150g/5oz golden granulated sugar

Method

Place the dandelion petals in a small saucepan over a low heat and pour over the boiling water. Bring to a simmer then immediately take off the heat and cover. Leave to steep for 12–24 hours. Strain through a jelly bag or muslin cloth and squeeze every last drop out.

Measure the liquid and match the volume with the same weight of sugar, for example 150ml/5fl oz liquid with 150g/5oz sugar. Pour the dandelion liquid and sugar into a saucepan and slowly heat until steaming, then continue to cook for 5–10 minutes. Leave to cool before pouring into a sterilised bottle: it will keep in the fridge for up to 3 months.

Dandelion Flower and Rum Cake

Serves 10–12

This golden, petal-flecked sponge cake is generously smothered with a cream cheese topping and laced with a splash of rum to bring out the mellow scent of dandelion flowers. Irresistible.

For the sponge

125g/4½oz butter

175g/6oz golden caster sugar

40 dandelion flowers, petals picked, plus extra petals to decorate

3 free-range eggs

175g/6oz plain flour, sifted

1 tsp baking powder, sifted

For the topping

40 dandelion flowers, petals picked

2–3 tbsp white rum

2 tbsp golden caster sugar

250g/9oz cream cheese

Method

Preheat the oven to 190°C/170°C fan/375°F and line a 20cm/8in cake tin with baking parchment.

Start by making the sponge. In a large bowl, beat together the butter and sugar until it turns pale. Add the petals picked from 40 dandelion flowers, then beat in the eggs one at a time. Finally, stir in the flour and baking powder, combine well and spoon into the cake tin. Bake for 35–40 minutes, or until a skewer pierced into the centre of the cake comes out clean. Turn out onto a cooling rack and leave to cool completely.

While the cake is cooling, make the topping. In a pestle and mortar, mash the petals with the rum and sugar and leave to infuse for a few minutes. Briefly strain the cream cheese of any excess liquid, then add to a bowl and and stir in the rum-infused petals. Taste and add more rum and sugar if needed.

Cover the top of the cake with the topping, cut into slices and serve. Alternatively, carefully cut the cake in half and spread half of the topping in the centre, then sandwich the two halves back together before smothering the rest on top. This cake is best eaten fresh, though you can store it in an airtight container at room temperature for up to 3 days: after a day or two, the rum will have evaporated a little and the dandelion flavour will pervade more.

Dandelion Meringues and Cream

Serves 4 | Gluten-free

The lightness of meringues and whipped cream complements the gentle flavour of dandelion petals flawlessly in this decadent dessert. You'll need to make the dandelion flower sugar a week or so in advance for the best results.

Ingredients

2 free-range egg whites

pinch of cornflour

150ml/5fl oz double cream

For the dandelion sugar

60 dandelion flowers, petals picked

80g/3oz golden caster sugar

Method

Prepare the dandelion sugar ahead of time. Mix the dandelion petals with the sugar in a small bowl, cover and leave for a minimum of 3 days or up to 2 weeks to infuse. Make sure the petals don't clump together too much, or tease them apart if they do.

Preheat the oven to 150°C/130°C fan/300°F and line a baking tray with baking parchment.

In a spotlessly clean bowl, whisk the egg whites into soft peaks, whisk in the cornflour and then whisk in three-quarters of the dandelion sugar a spoonful at a time, until glossy and thick.

Take a teaspoon of mixture and use a second teaspoon to ease it onto the baking parchment, pulling the spoon upwards to bring the mixture into a peak. Continue, spacing out the dollops across the baking tray, until all the mixture is used and you have about 16 meringues.

Bake in the middle of the oven for 30 minutes, then turn off the heat and leave with the oven door shut overnight or until the oven has completely cooled.

Put the remaining sugar mixture in a seed grinder, clean coffee grinder or pestle and mortar and grind to a fine texture.

Whisk the cream until it forms soft peaks. At this stage, you can either fold the powdered sugar mixture into the cream until well combined, or sprinkle on top when serving. To serve, divide the meringues between four plates and dollop the cream alongside. Alternatively, you can crush the meringues into the cream to make an Eton-mess-style dessert.

Any leftover meringues will keep well in an airtight container for a couple of weeks at room temperature or for 3 months in the freezer.

Dandelion Griddle Cakes

Makes approx. 20

I love the combination of bitter greens, juicy fruits and a biscuity base in these quick-to-cook and deceptively simple griddle cakes. They are delicious on their own, but you can also drizzle them with Dandelion Petal Syrup (p.63) for some extra, nutty sweetness.

Ingredients

100g/3½oz salted butter, plus extra for frying

½ tsp baking powder

225g/8oz plain flour, plus extra for dusting

75g/2¾oz soft brown sugar

50g/2oz raisins

20g/¾oz dandelion leaves, finely chopped or shredded

1 free-range egg

1–2 tsp milk or water (optional)

Dandelion Petal Syrup (p.63), to serve (optional)

Method

Add the butter, baking powder and flour to a food processor and process until the mixture resembles crumbs. To mix by hand, add the butter, baking powder and flour to a large bowl and rub together with your fingertips until it resemble crumbs.

Add the sugar, raisins, dandelion leaves and egg and, if needed, a splash of milk or water to help the mixture bind together. Combine well.

Roll out the dough on a lightly floured surface to about a 4mm/¼in thickness and use an 8cm/3¼in biscuit cutter or the rim of a glass to cut out about 20 cakes. Heat a griddle or heavy-bottomed frying pan over a medium heat and grease lightly with butter. When hot, add several of the cakes and cook for about 2 minutes on either side, or until golden brown. Repeat to cook all the cakes and enjoy warm or cold, drizzled with dandelion petal syrup, if you like.

These will keep, in an airtight container in the fridge, for up to 4 days.

Gorse

Ulex europaeus (Fabaceae)

I am always grateful for gorse's cheerful, unwavering presence on foraging walks – especially when the weather is harsh and biting. I will often pick a few fresh flowers to nibble on as I search for other plants, enjoying its delicate, slightly bitter taste. When the clouds disperse and the sun shines brightly, the flowers smell like coconut; inhale deeply next time you come across gorse and you'll see what I mean. When infused or dried, the flowers take on a floral scent more like green tea, making them an unusual and subtle ingredient to bake with.

There is a saying that 'when gorse is not in bloom, kissing is out of fashion'. Luckily for the romantics among us, this hardy, evergreen shrub is in brilliant yellow flower year round, though it's especially fragrant in spring. With its needle-like leaves, gorse provides a dense habitat for wildlife but poses a spiky challenge to foragers. It's also a hard plant to get rid of once it's established. Using the flowers for desserts is the perfect way to stop it seeding and taking over further. Native to Western Europe, Morocco and Algeria, it has now been introduced widely across the world.

Main identifying features

Grows up to 2m/6½ft tall as a dense evergreen shrub with green spikes and small, bright yellow flowers.

When to forage

Flowers are present all year round, but most abundant and fragrant in spring.

Where to forage

Grasslands, heathlands, parks, moors, scrublands, wastelands, open woods, coastal areas, cliff paths and, occasionally, in gardens.

How to forage

Carefully pick the flowers using gloves to avoid the spikes.

How to dry

100g/3½oz fresh flowers make around 25g/1oz dried. Spread the flowers out somewhere warm for a couple of days, or dry them in a dehydrator. Store in a sterilised jar out of direct sunlight for up to 6 months.

Cautions

In some countries such as Australia, New Zealand and areas of the US, gorse is invasive and often treated with pesticides in an attempt to eradicate it; do not eat the flowers if they've been sprayed with pesticides.

Other notable varieties
Western gorse (*Ulex gallii*)
Dwarf gorse (*Ulex minor*)

Gorse Flower Syrup

Makes 250ml/8½fl oz | Vegan and gluten-free

This syrup has a sweet moorland aroma and is very quick to make. Use it in Gorse Flower Oat Cookies (p.80), Genoise Sponges with Gorse Flower Cream (p.74) or dilute it to make a drink (or, of course, Gorsito Cocktails, p.76).

Ingredients

50g/2oz gorse flowers

125g/4½oz golden caster sugar

Method

Place the flowers and 250ml/8½fl oz water in a saucepan, bring to the boil and simmer for 10 minutes with the lid on. Strain through a sieve, making sure you squeeze all the liquid out. Clean the pan, then pour in the strained liquid, add the sugar and bring to a simmer, stirring to help the sugar dissolve. Simmer for a couple of minutes before pouring into a sterilised bottle. Store in the fridge for up to 4 months.

Genoise Sponges with Gorse Flower Cream

Makes 12 | Can be made gluten-free

These light, airy sponges topped with gorse-infused cream are simply divine. The credit for them goes to a friend's daughter, Jamila, who shared lots of great ideas for using gorse in sweet treats, including this one.

Ingredients

3 free-range eggs, separated

100g/3½oz golden granulated sugar

100g/3½oz rice flour (or plain flour, if not gluten-free), sifted

50g/2oz unsalted butter, melted and cooled

60ml/2fl oz Gorse Flower Syrup (p.73), plus extra for serving

For the topping

50g/2oz gorse flowers

200ml/6¾fl oz double cream

2 tbsp unrefined icing sugar, sifted

Method

Begin by making the topping. Place the gorse flowers in a small saucepan and pour over the cream. Stir over a low heat until steaming hot – take off the heat at the first sign of bubbling. Cover and leave for 20 minutes to an hour. Strain through a fine sieve or muslin cloth, discard the gorse flowers and leave to cool, then refrigerate.

Preheat the oven to 170°C/150°C fan/340°F and grease a 12-hole, non-stick muffin tin.

In a large, spotlessly clean bowl, whisk the egg whites to stiff peaks, sprinkle in half the golden granulated sugar and whisk till the mixture goes glossy.

In a smaller bowl, using an electric whisk, beat the remaining golden granulated sugar and the egg yolks at high speed until they are light, almost mousse-like and have grown considerably in size. Gently fold the egg yolk mixture into the egg white mixture, being careful to keep the light, airy texture. Then add half the flour, folding it in, then the remaining flour, followed by the melted butter. Combine well (but gently).

Divide the mixture evenly across the muffin-tin holes and bake for about 25 minutes, or until golden and a skewer in the centre of each cake comes out clean. Leave the cakes to cool for a few minutes before removing from the muffin tin and placing on a cooling rack; you may need to run a knife around each one to loosen them out of the tin. Using a teaspoon, drizzle each cake with the gorse flower syrup and set aside until completely cool.

Meanwhile, whip the cooled gorse cream to soft peaks and add the icing sugar, stirring well to combine. Place a healthy dollop of cream on top of each cake, drizzle with a little extra syrup, then enjoy immediately or keep for a few days in an airtight container in the fridge.

Gorsito Cocktails

Serves 2 | Vegan and gluten-free

Based on a mojito, this sweet rum cocktail tastes deliciously of gorse and is given a refreshing lift with the addition of mint. Created one night with a few friends around my kitchen table, it took a few tasting rounds to make sure this was the best combination. Thinking about it now, maybe we need to get together and test the recipe again.

Ingredients

1 lime

8 mint leaves (optional)

4 tbsp Gorse Flower Syrup (p.73)

50ml/1¾fl oz rum (see Tips)

ice cubes, to serve (with a few gorse petals frozen in, if you like)

gorse flowers, to decorate

For the powdered gorse sugar

1 dessertspoon dried gorse flowers (see drying instructions on p.70)

1 tsp golden caster sugar

Method

To make the powdered gorse sugar, combine the dried gorse flowers with the caster sugar and finely blend in a seed grinder or clean coffee grinder. Pour onto a saucer or flat plate.

Cut the lime in half and wet the rims of two cocktail glasses with one half, then dip the rims of the glasses in the sugar until coated.

Squeeze the juice from both lime halves into a jug or cocktail shaker. Tear the mint in half, if using, and slightly bruise the leaves in your hands to help release their minty aroma. Add to the jug or shaker along with the gorse flower syrup and rum, then stir or shake. Equally distribute between the glasses, followed by a couple of lime wedges and ice cubes. Sprinkle a few gorse flowers on top. Enjoy immediately.

Tips

For a stronger gorse flavour you can make gorse-infused rum. Pour approximately 200ml/6¾fl oz rum over 20g/¾oz gorse flowers, cover and leave for 2–3 days. Strain, discarding the flowers, and keep the rum in a sterilised bottle until needed.

If you don't want to go to the trouble of preparing the powdered gorse sugar, you could just use 1 tbsp golden caster sugar, instead.

Gorse and White Chocolate Truffles

Makes 15–20 | Gluten-free

Dressed like tempting bon-bons, these creamy truffles have a hint of coconut and are rolled in a subtle gorse flower sugar. I gave a box of these to my friend Amanda as a gift and they went down a treat.

Ingredients

175g/6oz white chocolate drops (or white chocolate bar, finely chopped)

3 heaped tbsp gorse petals, outer sepals and stem removed

3 tbsp double cream

25g/1oz desiccated coconut

For the gorse flower sugar

1 tbsp golden caster sugar or unrefined icing sugar

2 tbsp dried gorse flowers (see drying instructions on p.70)

Method

Place the chocolate in a heatproof bowl along with the gorse petals and cream and place over a saucepan of simmering water, ensuring that the water does not touch the bowl. Allow the chocolate to melt, then stir to check for lumps. Once smooth, immediately take it off the heat, mix in the desiccated coconut and place in the fridge for 1 hour to harden.

Meanwhile, make the gorse flower sugar by blitzing the sugar and dried gorse flowers in a spice grinder or clean coffee grinder until powdered, then place in a shallow bowl.

Take the mixture out of the fridge and, using a teaspoon and your hands, break off heaped teaspoons of the mixture, roll into balls, then roll in the sugar. Place in an airtight container (if keeping for a while) or serving dish. Sprinkle over any remaining gorse flower sugar and pop back in the fridge to harden again. Devour within 2 weeks. These are best eaten at room temperature.

Gorse Flower Oat Cookies

Makes 12

These wholemeal oat cookies are yummy just as they are, but rustically drizzling them with icing gives an extra gorse hit. As they're made using dried gorse flowers, you can bake up a batch at any time of year.

Ingredients

15g/½oz dried gorse flowers (see drying instructions on p.70)

75g/2¾oz butter

25g/1oz soft brown sugar

2 tbsp Gorse Flower Syrup (p.73)

75g/2¾oz rolled oats

75g/2¾oz wholemeal flour

For the icing (optional)

2 tbsp dried gorse flowers (see drying instructions on p.70)

2½ tbsp unrefined icing sugar

1 tbsp water or Gorse Flower Syrup (p.73)

Method

Preheat the oven to 180°C/160°C fan/350°F and grease a large non-stick baking tray.

Place the gorse flowers in a small saucepan along with the butter, brown sugar and gorse flower syrup. Heat, stirring occasionally, over a low heat, then, once the butter has melted, take off the heat and leave to infuse.

In a large bowl, mix the oats and wholemeal flour. Stir in the butter mixture and combine well. Roll into 12 small balls and flatten into cookies on the baking tray. Bake for 12–15 minutes, until golden and slightly crispy at the edges. Allow to cool completely before removing from the tray.

For the icing, if using, finely blend the flowers and sugar in a seed grinder or clean coffee grinder; the result should be a powder with tiny flecks of yellow. Mix in the water or gorse flower syrup. The consistency will be quite watery but leave to set for a few minutes before drizzling it over the cookies. Leave the icing to dry, then enjoy as wholesome sweet snacks; store in an airtight container, and eat within 1 week.

Summer

As bright, warm days arrive, so too do intoxicating colours and smells. Flower buds pop open, offering an outrageous assembly of colours, shapes and textures. Later in the season, they will fade and turn, but foragers need not focus on what we're losing: at summer's end, as stems hollow, there is a new intensity of spice captured in many sun-ripened, wild seeds.

Elderflowers

Sambucus nigra (Caprifoliaceae)

As summer arrives, soft and creamy flowerheads appear on the elder tree and their uplifting scent catches my attention. In folklore, elder is considered a protector, thought to ward off evil spirits, and I always think its knobbly wood has an ancient, mythical quality. The flowers meanwhile have antiviral properties that, when infused, will help guard against colds and flu. The best flowers are always (of course) just out of reach; if you're looking down at the flowerheads and there are none above you, you're probably standing by the wrong plant.

Elderflowers are best picked in full sun, when their delicate, floral fragrance is loveliest. Their flavour is complemented perfectly by citrus, so turning the flowerheads into elderflower cordial infused with lemon juice (p.90) is one of the best ways to capture their scent and lace it through desserts. As the season goes on, their smell becomes more pungent and they should be left to go to seed. Remember where you spotted them though, as the flowers will transform into a harvest of elderberries (p.178) in early autumn. Native to Europe, the common elder tree has also been introduced in Western Australia, Tasmania, areas of South America and North Africa.

Main identifying features

Grows up to 6m/20ft tall with a knobbly, cork-like trunk and branches. Leaves are dull green, long, serrated and pointed, growing opposite each other with one at the tip. Flowerheads are made up of many tiny, white flowers, and grow in a messy, uneven canopy.

When to forage

Late spring through to mid-summer.

Where to forage

Wastelands, parks, the edges of woods, roadsides, beside railways, scrublands and in hedges.

How to forage

Pick the flowerheads in full sun, when the flowers are open and smell sweet.

Cautions

The leaves and stems have a mild toxicity and shouldn't be eaten, while the raw flowers can give some people an upset stomach so it's best to infuse them.

Other notable varieties

Pink elder (*Sambucus nigra, f. porphyrophylla*)
American black elderberry (*Sambucus canadensis*)

Elderflower and Knotweed Fool

Serves 6 | Gluten-free

Softly whipped cream and sweet syrup blend perfectly with the slightly tart purée in this fool. Its lightness makes it the perfect finale to a rich, indulgent meal.

Ingredients

500g/1lb 2oz Japanese Knotweed Purée (p.44)

400ml/13½fl oz Elderflower Cordial (p.90)

400ml/13½fl oz cold whipping cream

Method

Heat the purée in a saucepan with a quarter of the cordial over a low heat and simmer gently for 10 minutes, stirring occasionally. Remove from the heat and put aside to cool completely.

Put the remaining cordial in a separate small saucepan and simmer over a low heat for 10–15 minutes until reduced to a more syrupy consistency. Remove from the heat and put aside to cool.

Whip the cream until it forms soft peaks and fold it into the cold purée. Spoon the mixture into elegant glasses or bowls and place in the fridge to chill for 1 hour or more. Swirl some of the elderflower syrup into each before serving.

Double Elderflower Jam Doughnuts

Makes 12

Doughnuts are a party food for me – when I'm tired and hungry from dancing, it's the smell of doughnuts that I sniff the air for. I created this recipe following a mini disaster: my Cornish town's annual festival and no doughnut van in sight. They are a delightful summery twist on the hot sugary ones I yearned for. Complete with a gorgeous soft, jam centre and sweet elderflower coating, these are melt-in-the-mouth with a double dose of elderflower.

Ingredients

135ml/4½fl oz milk

1 tbsp dried yeast

1 tbsp golden granulated sugar

50g/2oz butter, cubed and left to warm to room temperature

275g/9½oz plain flour (you can replace 25g/1oz with wholemeal flour, if you wish), sifted, plus extra for dusting

1 free-range egg, beaten

300–500ml/10–18fl oz vegetable oil, for frying

240g/8¾oz Elderflower and Greengage Jam (p.91)

For the glaze

4 tbsp unrefined icing sugar, sifted

2–3 tbsp Elderflower Cordial (p.90)

Method

Warm the milk in a small saucepan over a low heat until lukewarm. Add 2 tablespoons of the warm milk to a small jug with the yeast and a pinch of the sugar, mix, then leave until frothy.

Meanwhile, gently plop the butter cubes into the remaining milk, mixing until the butter dissolves.

In a large bowl, add the flour and remaining sugar, make a well in the middle and add the frothy yeast, buttery milk and the egg. Mix, then knead and stretch for 5 minutes, either in the bowl or on a clean, flour-dusted surface. Place back in the bowl, cover, and leave in a warm spot for 1 hour or until doubled in size.

Knead the dough for another 5 minutes, then dust a large baking tray with flour. Break the dough into 12 pieces, roll each piece into a ball and place on the tray. Cover with a clean tea towel and leave to rise for 30 minutes or until doubled in size.

Place some kitchen paper on a couple of dinner plates (2 sheets on each) and heat the oil in a deep saucepan, no more than half full, to 150°C/300°F or until a small piece of dough dropped in the oil sizzles and floats to the surface. Using a slotted spoon, drop 2–4 dough balls into the oil, fry until golden brown, then turn over and brown on the other side. Remove onto the kitchen paper, then repeat with the remaining dough balls.

Next make the glaze. In a shallow bowl, mix the icing sugar and cordial together. Dip each side of each doughnut in the mixture, then place on a cooling rack. The doughnuts can be filled with jam while still hot or allowed to cool first.

To fill, use a teaspoon or filling nozzle to make a small slot in the side of each doughnut and fill with 2 teaspoons of jam. Dip each doughnut in the coating for a final time before eating. These are best eaten fresh, but will keep for 3 days: store in an airtight container.

Elderflower Cordial

Makes 1½ litres/2¾ pints
Vegan and gluten-free

To me, this delicately flavoured cordial conjures up the feeling of a warm summer breeze and long, lazy days. Floral, light and citrussy, it is used in all the recipes in this section.

Ingredients

25 elderflower heads

500g/1lb 2oz golden granulated sugar

1½ litres/2¾ pints boiling water

2 unwaxed lemons

50g/2oz citric acid (optional, this helps preserve and gives a stronger tart flavour: if not using citrid acid, add one extra lemon)

Method

Check the elderflowers for bugs, then, over a large plate, pull the stalks through a fork to remove the petals. Pick off any remaining flowers by hand, then discard the stems.

Place the sugar in a large saucepan and pour the boiling water over, stirring until dissolved. Place the elderflowers in a clean bucket or large, heatproof bowl and pour the hot sugared water over them.

Slice the lemons into quarters, squeeze the juice into the bucket then add the squeezed lemon quarters and the citric acid, if using. Stir, cover and leave for 24–48 hours, stirring occasionally. Strain the mixture through a sieve, or preferably a fine muslin cloth, and funnel into sterilised bottles. The cordial will keep for up to 2 months in the fridge without citric acid, or for up to 9 months with it.

Tip

You can also swap out one of the lemons in this recipe for an orange to make an Elderflower and Orange Cordial – my favourite adaptation of this drink. Cut 1 unwaxed orange into wedges, squeeze the juice into the bucket, then add the wedges along with the lemon and 4 tablespoons of orange juice. If not using citric acid, add 2 tablespoons of lemon juice, too.

Elderflower and Greengage Jam

Makes 350–400g/12–14oz
Vegan and gluten-free

Towards the end of summer, I often spot ripe greengages – a member of the plum family – in my local grocer's. With just enough tartness to balance the subtle, floral mood of elderflowers, this jam goes perfectly with cheese and crackers. Though to be honest, I more often make it as a filling for doughnuts (p.88): in these sugary, deep-fried treats I feel it has found its perfect home.

Ingredients

300g/10oz greengages, stones removed and chopped (approx. 325–450g/11½oz–1lb whole fruit)

90ml/3fl oz Elderflower Cordial (see opposite page)

225g/8oz golden granulated sugar

Method

Add the chopped greengages to a small saucepan with the elderflower cordial. Bring to a simmer, then cook over a low heat for 10–15 minutes, or until the fruits become mushy and soft and have completely broken down.

Strain through a sieve, pushing through as much pulp as you can and discarding the skins.

Place the sieved pulp mixture back into the saucepan, adding the sugar and stirring until dissolved. Turn the heat up to medium–high until the jam reaches 105°C/221°F on a sugar thermometer or the mixture thickens to jam consistency (you can use the 'setting test' to double check this, if you like: see Tip on p.172). Be careful not to burn the bottom. Pour into a sterilised jar and immediately screw on the lid, then store. Once opened, keep in the fridge for up to 6 months.

Tip

Greengages ripen in late summer. If you don't have them in your area, you can use pears instead. To do this, blend 300g/10oz peeled and cored pears (approx. 450g/1lb whole fruit) with the cordial first, until completely smooth, then add to the pan along with the sugar. Heat over a low heat until the sugar has dissolved, then turn the heat up to medium–high until the jam reaches 105°C/221°F on a sugar thermometer or thickens to jam consistency. Store as above.

Elderflower and Carrageen Refreshers

Serves 4 | Vegan and gluten-free

Somewhere between a jelly and a cool summer drink, these refreshers (or 'slurpers' as photographer Elliott calls them!) have a soothing texture created by the natural thickening quality of the carrageen seaweed. The combination of elderflower and carrageen gives them beneficial antiviral qualities for coughs and colds, too.

Ingredients

20g/¾oz dried carrageen seaweed (see Tip)

250ml/8½fl oz Elderflower Cordial (p.90), plus 1 dessertspoon

200g/7oz summer fruits (e.g. raspberries, strawberries, grapes or blueberries)

Method

Cover the carrageen with cold water and leave to soak for 10 minutes. Drain and rinse before transferring to a medium saucepan, adding 500ml/18fl oz water and the 250ml/8½fl oz elderflower cordial. Bring to the boil over a medium heat, then turn down the heat and simmer for 20 minutes.

Strain the mixture through a jelly bag or fine sieve into a large jug or bowl, then pour in the extra dessertspoon of cordial and leave to cool to room temperature.

Roughly chop the fruits and distribute evenly among four 200ml/6¾fl oz glasses. Pour the strained and cooled liquid over the fruits and refrigerate for a few hours before serving.

Tip

Carrageen *(Chondrus crispus)*, also known as Irish moss, is available in health-food stores and from online seaweed suppliers. Buy the sun-bleached, whole seaweed rather than processed powder.

Mint

Mentha arvensis (Lamiaceae)

Finding wild mint is magic. I've often caught its distinct scent in the air mid-walk and wandered off the path to find an abundant patch of this menthol-tasting, cooling herb. Fresh, wild mint is far superior to the dried stuff; be it the most commonly known field mint (*Mentha arvensis*), spicy peppermint (*Mentha piperita*), gentle, furry-leaved apple mint (*Mentha suaveolens*), sharp spearmint (*Mentha spicata*) or earthy water mint (*Mentha aquatica*). Mint certainly knows how to spread, often escaping gardens to seed itself in the wild; if you find some growing, the chances are there'll be more lurking nearby. Many types naturally hybridise, too (like the hybridised water mint, pictured right), creating new minty blends.

Mint is pretty cosmopolitan; it's native to Europe, North America, Asia and much of Australasia and Africa and has been introduced to parts of South America, too. As a gentle digestive aid, it is perfect as an after-dinner treat or infused into a soothing tea. It can also act as a tonic for coughs and colds, reduce fevers and, of course, freshen the breath. What better way to finish a meal?

Main identifying features

Grows up to 1m/3ft tall. Serrated leaves grow opposite each other in pairs, some varieties' leaves are furry, others smooth. Flowers are lilac to pinkish in colour, growing either in clusters up the stems or in spikes of flowerheads at the tips.

When to forage

Leaves can be picked from late spring, flowers appear later in summer.

Where to forage

Damp and boggy ground near ponds, riverbanks, streams, ditches and marshes and in wet woodland, wastelands and roadsides. It also has a reputation of spreading in gardens if not contained in a pot.

How to forage

Pick the leaves off the stem, or pick sprigs and stems of leaves and flowers to decorate.

Other notable varieties

Peppermint (*Mentha piperita*)
Apple mint (*Mentha suaveolens*)
Spearmint (*Mentha spicata*)
Water mint (*Mentha aquatica*)

Chocolate Mint Leaves

Makes 10–15 | Vegan and gluten-free

Move over after-dinner mints: simply dipping fresh mint leaves in melted chocolate creates a more divine end to a meal than a box of chocolates ever could. It's best to use freshly cut leaves, dip them twice in the chocolate to create a deliciously crisp coating, and enjoy them within a couple of days. I serve these leaves as a vegan alternative to my Mint Chocolate Truffles (p.102).

Ingredients

10–15 mint leaves (depending on size, see Tip)

30g/1oz vegan dark chocolate

Method

Break the chocolate into squares and place in a heatproof bowl over a small saucepan of simmering water. Do not let the water touch the bowl. Lay out a piece of baking parchment on a large baking tray.

As the chocolate melts, take a single leaf by the stem and drag it through the chocolate. Drag a second time for a thicker, crisper coating. Place to dry on the baking paper and repeat with all the mint leaves. Once the chocolate has set, store in an airtight container in the fridge and eat within a couple of days.

Tip

You may need more chocolate or leaves depending on how thick you'd like the chocolate and the size of the leaves. You really can tailor these to your taste.

Mint and Coconut Fridge Cake

Serves 8–12 | Vegan and gluten-free

I invented this recipe on a hot summer day when I was craving something refreshingly cool with a tinge of sweetness. I wanted to avoid the heaviness of dairy, and although rich, this cake is both light and indulgent, and hits the spot.

Ingredients

200g/7oz cashew nuts

60g/2¼oz desiccated coconut

4 tbsp coconut oil

2 tbsp maple syrup

40–50 mint leaves (to taste)

For the base

2 tbsp coconut oil

100g/3½oz pitted dates, chopped

pinch of sea salt (optional)

100g/3½oz ground almonds

Method

Put the cashew nuts in a bowl, cover with water and soak for up to 4 hours. If you've less time, pour boiling water over them and leave for at least 1 hour.

Meanwhile, grease and line a 23cm/9in cake tin, ideally loose-bottomed, with baking parchment.

If using a food processor, prepare the fridge cake base by tipping in all of the base ingredients and blitzing together until a sticky dough forms. Alternatively, warm the 2 tablespoons of coconut oil in a small saucepan, then take off the heat, stir in the dates and salt, if using, and put aside for 10 minutes. Add the ground almonds and, using clean hands (I find this gets better results than a wooden spoon), rub the mixture together until the dates have broken down and you have a sticky dough. Press the mixture into the tin to make an even base, then place the tin in the fridge.

Strain the cashew nuts, discarding the water, then place in a food processor with the remaining ingredients (or use a stick blender) and blitz until smooth. Test the flavour and blend in more mint leaves, if you like, to taste. Spoon the topping onto the base and carefully smooth over. Place in the fridge for a couple of hours and remove just before serving. Store in the fridge for up to 5 days, or freeze for up to 2 months (if the latter, just wait 10 minutes before slicing, then enjoy cold).

Mint and White Chocolate Muffins

Makes 9

These substantial muffins have chunks of white chocolate speckled through them and a delightful minty tang. If your palate craves something sweeter, simply drizzle on the optional icing.

Ingredients

20–30 mint leaves (double if small or mild leaves)

100ml/3½fl oz single or pouring cream

20g/¾oz unsalted butter

125g/4½oz golden granulated sugar

175g/6½oz plain flour, sifted

25g/1oz wholemeal flour (or use all plain if you prefer), sifted

2 tsp baking powder, sifted

2 tbsp cornflour, sifted

3 free-range eggs

100g/3½oz white chocolate chips (or white chocolate bar, chopped)

For the icing (optional)

25 mint leaves, finely shredded

2 tbsp boiling water

100g/3½oz unrefined icing sugar, sifted

Method

For the muffins, finely chop the 20–30 mint leaves and immediately place in a small saucepan with the cream, butter and half the golden granulated sugar. Bring to a gentle boil over a low heat, then take off the heat and set aside to cool.

Meanwhile, preheat the oven to 170°C/150°C fan/340°F and prepare 9 holes of a muffin tin with paper cupcake cases.

Place the flours, baking powder and cornflour in a large bowl.

When the cream mixture is cool, stir in the remaining granulated sugar, then beat in the eggs. Pour the wet ingredients into the dry and combine, making sure all the flour is mixed in. Stir in the chocolate chips (or chopped chocolate), then spoon into the cases until each is two-thirds full. Bake for 25 minutes or until golden on top. Place on a cooling rack and allow to cool completely.

If making the icing, place the mint leaves in a small bowl and pour over the boiling water. Mash together and leave to sit for a few minutes. Add the icing sugar into the mint leaves, stirring until it makes a smooth paste. You might need to add a little bit more water, though you don't want the icing too watery. Spoon over the muffins and leave to set. Eat fresh or store in an airtight container in the fridge for up to 4 days.

Mint Chocolate Truffles

Makes approx. 20 | Gluten-free

I like to take a large bite of one of these perfectly textured truffles and wait until its minty taste arrives on my tongue. Even their uneven spherical shape gives me a thrill; there really is nothing like homemade truffles.

Ingredients

20–30 mint leaves (depending on leaf size)

150ml/5fl oz double cream, plus a little extra

50g/2oz dark chocolate, finely chopped

75g/2¾oz milk chocolate, finely chopped

1–2 tbsp cacao powder

Method

Roughly chop the mint leaves and immediately place in a small saucepan with the cream. Bring to an almost boil (the cream should be quivering, not boiling) over a low heat, then remove from the heat and allow to steep for 30 minutes or longer. Strain every last drop of the cream through a jelly bag or fine sieve, measure and, if needed, add more cream to make up to 125ml/4¼fl oz. Pour the strained cream back in the saucepan and set aside.

Add the chopped dark and milk chocolate to a medium bowl. Heat the cream for a second time over a low heat, until hot and quivering once more, then pour over the chocolate. Leave for 1 minute before whisking from the centre outwards until the chocolate and cream make a smooth blend. Cover and place in the fridge for 6 hours or overnight to create a firm ganache.

Using a teaspoon, break off pieces of ganache and roll between your finger and palm to make 5cm/2in balls before placing on a baking tray lined with baking parchment. This stage will be messy as the ganache softens in your hands and the mixture won't naturally want to roll into a ball – persevere and be willing to accept odd shapes rather than perfect spheres. Return the tray of truffles to the fridge for 1 hour. Place the cacao powder in a shallow bowl and roll the truffles in the powder until evenly covered.

These truffles keep for up to 2 weeks in the fridge and are perfect to give as a gift or to enjoy after dinner, relaxing on the sofa.

Rose Petals

Rosa rugosa (Rosaceae)

I have fond childhood memories of walking around my granny's garden smelling the roses; luckily for her, I didn't know they were edible then. When I spot their vivid blooms in parks, gardens or wild areas, I still love to stop and breathe in their aroma, especially in the evenings when that heady, floral scent seems strongest.

Roses are a plant of contrasts: associated with love and softness, but flowering off viciously thorny stems. Worldwide, there are several hundred wild species, which typically have five petals and bloom just once a year with a strong perfume, making them the best fragrant varieties to use for food and drinks. My favourites for desserts are Japanese roses (*Rosa rugosa*), which are often planted in gardens or grow wild near the beach, hence their nickname: 'beach roses'. Native to Central China, Japan and Korea, they have been introduced to North America and Europe. And lucky for us they have: rose infusions are good for anxiety and for calming upset stomachs, not to mention they taste pretty good, too.

Main identifying features

Grows up to 1½m/5ft tall with thorny stems. Roses with open, five-petalled flowers are the most fragrant varieties and have pink, white or purple flowers and smooth or slightly ridged leaves.

When to forage

Early to late summer when the flowers are fully in bloom and petals come away easily.

Where to forage

Wastelands, parks, gardens, hedges, beaches, the edges of woods, roadsides and scrublands.

How to forage

Collect recently fallen petals, or petals that come away easily in your hand. There's no need to pick the whole flowerhead; keeping it intact ensures rosehip fruits (p.208) will grow later in the year.

How to dry

60g/2oz fresh petals make approximately 15g/½oz dried. Dry in a dehydrator according to manufacturer's instructions, or spread out somewhere warm for 48 hours. Store in a sterilised jar out of direct sunlight for up to 6 months.

Cautions

Mind those thorns! And avoid plants sprayed with pesticides.

Other notable varieties

As well as wild roses, you can also use many cultivated varieties of the *Rosa* species – opt for fragrant ones.

Rose Water

Makes approx. 500ml/18fl oz
Vegan and gluten-free

Rose water is a satisfying and simple way to capture the flavour and colour of different roses and I take great pleasure in bottling their uniqueness. Use in Iced Rose Shortbreads (p.111) and Fennel, Rose and Almond Milk Puddings (p.141) or splash on your bare face as a skin refresher!

Ingredients

700ml/1¼ pints fresh rose petals (approx. 75g/3oz gently pressed down)

Method

Chop the rose petals and place in a jug, packing the petals down as tightly as possible. Pour over just enough boiling water to cover the petals. If petals float to the top, be sure to stir them back in.

Cover the jug and set aside for 24–48 hours. Strain the liquid through a muslin cloth into sterilised bottles, making sure you squeeze out every drop of the rose water and store in the fridge for a week, or freeze in an ice cube tray and defrost amounts as needed.

Rose Syrup

Makes approx. 500ml/18fl oz
Vegan and gluten-free

This is pure rose syrup, for those who get excited about rose petals and their smell. You can drizzle it over any dessert you choose, dilute it to make a calming drink or use it to make Rose and Watermelon Granita (p.112).

Ingredients

225g/8oz golden granulated sugar

500ml/18fl oz Rose Water (see above)

Method

Add the sugar and rose water to a saucepan and heat over a low heat, stirring until the sugar has dissolved; do not boil. Leave over a low heat for 20 minutes or until the liquid doesn't look watery (it will become syrupy when cooled).

Leave to cool, then pour into sterilised bottles and store for a couple of weeks in the fridge, or freeze in portions.

Shocking Pink Rose Sponge

Serves 10

This cake looks like a classic sponge cake, but the twist is it's sandwiched together with the zingiest, freshest wild rose preserve you've ever tasted. The preserve recipe was given to me by fellow forager Emma Gunn, and can be made up to six months in advance.

Ingredients

250g/9oz butter, softened

250g/9oz soft brown sugar

4 free-range eggs

250g/9oz self-raising flour (or 250g/9oz plain flour plus 3 tsp baking powder)

For the rose preserve

30g/1oz pink, fragrant rose petals

85g/3oz golden caster sugar

1 tbsp lemon juice

For the topping (optional)

1 tbsp dried rose petals (see drying instructions on p.104)

1 dessertspoon soft brown sugar

pink, fragrant rose petals, to decorate

Method

First make the preserve by adding the rose petals, golden caster sugar and lemon juice to a blender and blending until it resembles a smooth purée. You can use it immediately or store in a sterilised jar in the fridge for up to 6 months.

Preheat the oven to 180°C/160°C fan/350°F and line two 20cm/8in loose-bottomed cake tins with baking parchment.

In a large bowl, beat together the butter, the 250g/9oz soft brown sugar and 1 teaspoon of the rose preserve until light and creamy. Add the eggs one at a time, beating each one in thoroughly, then fold in the flour. Spoon equal amounts into the cake tins and bake in the middle of the oven for 20–25 minutes. The cakes are ready when they start separating from the side of the tins and spring back when touched.

Remove from the oven and leave for 5 minutes before turning out onto a cooling rack. Once the sponges have cooled, spread the preserve onto the top of one, making sure you spread right to the edges before placing the other sponge on top.

If making the topping, grind the dried rose petals and sugar in a seed grinder or clean coffee grinder until it resembles icing sugar, then sprinkle over the top of the cake. Decorate with fresh rose petals.

This cake will keep well for up to 5 days in an airtight container at room temperature.

Iced Rose Shortbreads

Makes 20–25

A very sweet, rosy treat that tastes heavenly as it melts in your mouth, I love these biscuits dipped in the floral icing – though my mum can never resist them long enough to ice them, and tells me they're delicious even without.

Ingredients

225g/8oz butter, softened

50g/2oz golden caster sugar

275g/9½oz plain flour, sifted, plus extra for dusting

50g/2oz cornflour, sifted

25g/1oz rose petals (fresh or freshly discarded from the Rose Water on p.107), finely chopped

For the icing (optional)

90ml/3fl oz Rose Water (p.107)

200g/7oz unrefined icing sugar, sifted

Method

Preheat the oven to 170°C/150°C fan/340°F and grease two large baking trays.

In a large bowl, beat the butter and caster sugar together. Little by little add the flour and cornflour, mixing in as you go. Add the chopped rose petals and stir into the mix.

Lightly flour a clean surface and rolling pin and roll out the mixture until 3–4mm/⅛in thick, then use a biscuit cutter (one of around 7cm/2¾in works well) to cut out the shortbreads. Fill the baking trays; you won't need much space between each biscuit, as they won't rise. Bake for 30 minutes or until lightly golden. Carefully transfer to a cooling rack – they can be quite delicate – and leave until completely cold before icing (if you are).

Once the shortbread are cool, pour the rose water into a bowl and the icing sugar into a separate bowl or wide plate. Using a flat, slotted spatula, very briefly dip each shortbread into the rose water; allow to drip for a few seconds before carefully tossing in the icing sugar and placing on a wire rack for a few hours to dry.

Once completely dried, store in an airtight container and eat within a week. They also freeze well.

Rose and Watermelon Granita

Makes approx. 1 litre/1¾ pints
Vegan and gluten-free

Matching colours of rose and watermelon make this a vibrant granita for both the eyes and taste buds. I created it one day in my sun-filled kitchen, when I was working from home and daydreaming about going for a long walk and smelling the roses. Having made some Rose Syrup (p.107) the week before, this sorbet was the perfect restoring antidote for time spent indoors and remains a favourite of mine.

Ingredients

1kg/2lb 3oz watermelon flesh, deseeded and roughly chopped

125ml/4¼fl oz Rose Syrup (p.107)

Method

Place the chopped watermelon in a blender and blend until smooth. Strain into a bowl through a fine sieve to remove any stray seeds and stir in the rose syrup.

Pour into a 1½-litre/2¾-pint lidded, freezer-proof container and freeze for 30 minutes to 1 hour or until ice crystals start forming around the edges. Remove from the freezer and mash the edges with a fork. Return to the freezer for a further hour, then repeat the mashing before leaving it to freeze overnight.

Take out of the freezer 20 minutes before you are ready to serve, then scoop into chilled dishes.

Yarrow

Achillea millefolium (Asteraceae)

Yarrow was one of the first wild herbs I got to know – learning of its ability to treat wounds (hence its common nicknames, 'bleedwort' or 'woundwort') as well as its helpfulness in soothing colds and bringing down fevers. I love pointing it out in people's lawn, where it often grows unseen. In wilder areas where it has been allowed to flower and bloom, the scent is like honey in the hot summer sun. Its leaves are gorgeously aromatic and herbal when rubbed or infused, reminiscent of lavender.

Named after Achilles in Latin, the legendary Greek warrior, yarrow is strong in many ways. It has firm, upright stems and thrives in harsh environments (including the most manicured of lawns). It bounces back, even after been regularly mowed, and has powerful medicinal qualities as well as containing vitamins A and C, potassium, zinc, magnesium, calcium, phosphorus and niacin. Native to Europe, North America, North Asia and much of the Middle East, it has been introduced to South America and areas of South Asia.

Main identifying features

Grows up to 50cm/1½ft tall with long feathery leaves and furred, dry stems. The tight flowerheads have white (sometimes pinkish) petals and pale, yellow centres.

When to forage

Flowers appear in early summer and die back in early autumn.

Where to forage

Exposed landscapes including garden lawns, dry grassy banks, wastelands, fields, hedgerows, mountain sides and sand dunes.

How to forage

Pick the long, fresh leaves from ground level (not the small ones on the flower stems) and cut off the flowerheads with scissors as the stems are strong.

How to dry

Loosely tie yarrow stems and leaves into a bundle and hang or lie them in a warm place for a few days: 100g/3½oz fresh leaves or flowers will make around 35g/1oz dried. Once dry, chop them up and store them in a sterilised jar.

Cautions

This plant can cause skin irritation for some, and shouldn't be handled in large amounts or for long periods of time. Avoid picking in lawns treated with weedkiller.

When collecting yarrow, pick the long, fresh leaves that grow from ground level rather than those on the stem.

Yarrow Crème Brûlée

Serves 4 | Gluten-free

A thick, creamy custard is infused with yarrow in this not-too-sweet dessert, and its irresistibly crunchy, brûléed topping also has a wild yarrow twist. As it's prepared with dried yarrow, it can be made any time of year.

Ingredients

400ml/13½fl oz double cream

10g/⅓oz (around 3 heaped tbsp) dried and chopped yarrow leaves and flowers (see drying instructions on p.114)

3 large free-range egg yolks

1 tbsp soft brown sugar

For the caramel topping

1 heaped dessertspoon dried and chopped yarrow leaves (see drying instructions on p.114)

75ml/2½fl oz boiling water

100g/3½oz golden caster sugar

Method

Pour the cream into a small saucepan and pop in the chopped, dried yarrow leaves and flowers. Bring to a simmer over a low heat, then take off the heat and leave to infuse for 20 minutes before straining through a jelly bag or muslin cloth. Give the jelly bag a good squeeze so you extract all the aroma you can, then pour the cream back into the (cleaned) pan.

Combine the yolks and soft brown sugar in a bowl, then add to the cream. Stir continuously over a low heat until the mixture thickens enough to coat the back of a spoon. The mixture will become more solid when cooled, so don't worry too much if it seems a little runny at this stage.

Pour into 4 small ramekins or glasses and leave to set in the fridge for a few hours or overnight.

Meanwhile, make the caramel topping. Put the chopped, dried yarrow leaves in a small bowl and pour over the boiling water. Cover and leave to infuse and cool for at least an hour or overnight.

Once cool, strain the water, discarding the leaves, then pour it into a small saucepan. Add the golden caster sugar, stir, and bring to the boil. Here, you have the choice of a light brown, caramelised topping with a mild herby flavour, which is ready when the syrup measures 130°C/266°F on a sugar thermometer. Alternatively you can go for the traditional 'burnt sugar' where it will turn a dark brown colour and will be about 138°C/280°F on a sugar thermometer, but you won't be able to taste the yarrow in the topping! Boil the syrup, without stirring, until it reaches one of these temperatures. The choice is yours...

Pour a thin layer of the syrup over each custard-filled vessel and swirl around to evenly distribute, then leave to cool for 1 hour. Serve the same day, or the caramel will start to dissolve again.

Yarrow Flower Syrup

Makes 550ml/19¾fl oz
Vegan and gluten-free

From the moment the flowers are steeped in hot water, I fall in love with the scent of this syrup. It smells almost like menthol – or is it liquorice? I can't quite make up my mind. A pleasant drink when diluted with water, it's also an essential ingredient in Yarrow Flower Ice Cream (below).

Ingredients

30g/1oz yarrow flowers, chopped

450ml/15¼fl oz boiling water

300g/10oz light brown sugar

Method

Place the chopped flowers in a heatproof bowl and pour the boiling water over them. Cover and leave overnight or for 24 hours.

Strain the liquid through a sieve into a saucepan, add the sugar and gently heat, stirring, until the sugar has dissolved. Bring to the boil and simmer for 10 minutes before leaving to cool, then decant into sterilised bottles. Keeps for up to 3 months in the fridge.

Yarrow Flower Ice Cream

Makes 500ml/18fl oz | Gluten-free

Butterscotch-tinted with a lingering hint of yarrow, I find this soft ice cream divinely comforting. I love eating it simply scooped into a waffle cone so I can savour its subtle flavour.

Ingredients

150ml/5fl oz double cream

40g/1½oz unrefined icing sugar, sifted

150ml/5fl oz Yarrow Flower Syrup (see above)

2 free-range egg whites

Method

Beat the cream and icing sugar in a bowl until stiff, then stir in the yarrow flower syrup.

In a separate, spotlessly clean bowl, whisk the egg whites until they form stiff peaks, then fold them into the cream mixture until combined.

Transfer the mixture to an ice cream maker and churn according to the manufacturer's instructions. Alternatively, pour into a 750ml–1-litre/1⅓–1¾-pint lidded, freezer-proof container, seal and freeze for 1–2 hours. Remove from the freezer, stir well to ensure the syrup is evenly combined, then pop back in the freezer to set completely. It will keep for up to 2 months.

Yarrow and Honey Mule

Serves 4 | Gluten-free and dairy-free

The smell of honey-scented yarrow flowers one hot summer day inspired this medicinal take on a mule cocktail. Not only does it taste good, but it helps soothe coughs and colds. Adding fresh yarrow leaves and ginger will give the cocktail an extra 'zing', but it is still pretty punchy without them. My friend Antonia and I enjoyed these one evening in her allotment – it felt appropriate surrounded by herbs and flowers – and they made the cycle home quite interesting, too!

Ingredients

4 tbsp yarrow leaves, taken off the stem and chopped (optional)

1 tsp lemon juice

1 tsp grated fresh ginger (optional)

125ml/4¼fl oz vodka, plus 1 tsp

100ml/3½fl oz Yarrow Flower Syrup (p.120)

1 tbsp honey

400ml/13½fl oz sparkling water

To serve

ice cubes

lemon slices

Method

In a pestle and mortar, mash together the yarrow leaves, if using, lemon juice, grated ginger, if using, and 1 teaspoon of vodka.

Pour the yarrow flower syrup and remaining vodka into a jug, add the honey and stir until dissolved. Add the mashed yarrow-leaf blend, if using, and the sparkling water, then pour into glasses garnished with ice and lemon slices.

Pineapple Weed

Matricaria discoidea (Asteraceae)

This persistent plant thrives in well-trodden areas in the city and countryside, hence its nickname: street weed. Rubbing the flowers releases their smell, which is reminiscent of pineapple, mango or even passionfruit – a joyous discovery for adults and little ones alike. As children, friends and I would mix these sweet-smelling flowers into experimental, homemade perfumes.

Also known as 'wild chamomile' or 'false chamomile', pineapple weed shares the medicinal and herbal qualities of chamomile (*Chamaemelum nobile* and *Matricaria chamomilla*), with the addition of a fruity flavour. It's distinguished by its petal-less, pineapple-shaped flowerheads, which are also thought to have inspired its name. It has analgesic properties and can numb pain; it's often used to treat insomnia, or rubbed on insect bites and used to soothe irritated skin (though beware, some people are allergic to it). Native to North America, it has been well-established in Europe since the 19th century and has spread across much of Asia and Australia. It's often infused to make a caffeine-free tea, but I think sweet treats show off its flavour to far greater effect.

Main identifying features

Grows to 12cm/5in tall with feathery leaves and greeny-yellow, domed flowerheads with no petals.

When to forage

Early summer to early autumn when in flower.

Where to forage

Pineapple weed thrives where people, vehicles and animals tread: it's most often found in the dry, compacted soil of pathways, pavement cracks, field edges and driveways.

How to forage

Use scissors to snip off the flowerheads as the stems are hardy.

How to dry

Place in a sunny room or warm outdoor spot for 1–2 days until dry, or use a dehydrator. To replace fresh pineapple weed with dried in recipes, use about a quarter of the weight given and make up the rest of the weight with water.

Cautions

Can cause an allergic reaction in some people; symptoms may be similar to hay fever or include skin or eye irritation. May cause stomach upsets if consumed in large amounts.

Pineapple Weed Syrup

Makes 500ml/18fl oz | Vegan and gluten-free

Hand on heart, this is the best pineapple weed syrup you'll ever try: aromatic and citrussy. The secret is to discard the green bits and just use the flowerheads. It's delicious drizzled over yoghurt, diluted for drinks or used in Pineapple Weed and Coconut Ice Lollies (p.132).

Ingredients

150g/5oz pineapple weed flowerheads (no stalks)

250g/9oz golden granulated sugar

2 tbsp pineapple juice

Method

Place the flowerheads and 500ml/18fl oz water in a small saucepan and simmer over a low heat for 5 minutes, then leave to cool. Strain through a jelly bag or fine sieve, squeezing out all the liquid you can, then discard the flowerheads and add the liquid back into the pan along with the sugar and pineapple juice. Bring to a simmer over a low heat, stirring, and cook for a further 3 minutes. Store in a sterilised bottle in the fridge for up to 3 months.

Pineapple Weed Preserve

Makes 400g/14oz | Vegan and gluten-free

Sticky, fruity and floral, this preserve pairs pineapple weed flowers with pineapple fruit to make a highly addictive mixture. It's gorgeous blended with yoghurt in Pineapple Weed Filo Tarts (p.131) and as a sticky centre in Pineapple Weed Oat Slices (p.128).

Ingredients

150g/5oz fresh or canned pineapple

175ml/6fl oz unsweetened pineapple juice (I use the juice from canned pineapple)

160g/5½oz pineapple weed flowerheads (no stalks)

250g/9oz golden granulated sugar

Method

Add the pineapple and pineapple juice to a food processor and blend until the chunks are broken into small pieces. Add to a medium saucepan along with the flowerheads and sugar.

Simmer over a low heat for about 30 minutes, or until the liquid is almost completely absorbed and the mixture falls heavily off a spoon in blobs. Store in a sterilised jar in the fridge for up to 6 months.

Pineapple Weed Oat Slices

Makes 9 | Vegan and gluten-free

With their crumbly oat topping, chewy pineapple weed centre and moist base, these oat slices are so moreish that my friend H once ate four of them for dessert as we sat on his boat one summer evening. They also make a great breakfast treat.

Ingredients

300g/10oz oats, gluten-free if needed (I use half jumbo rolled oats, half porridge oats)

300g/10oz Pineapple Weed Preserve (p.127)

125ml/4¼fl oz vegetable oil

3–5 tbsp boiling water

Method

Preheat the oven to 150°C/130°C fan/300°F and grease a square 20cm/8in cake tin.

In a large mixing bowl, place the oats, one-third of the preserve and the oil, combine well, then gradually add the boiling water until the mixture sticks together (you may not need to use all the water). Spoon two-thirds of the oat mixture into the tin and press into an even layer.

Use a teaspoon to dot the remaining preserve across the oats, then carefully spread to join up the dots and create a sweet layer. Evenly spread the remaining oat mixture on top and press it down firmly with the back of a spoon. Bake for 40 minutes and leave to cool before slicing into squares.

Pineapple Weed Filo Tarts

Makes 12

I love the lightness of these fruity, aromatic baked tarts. Creating a perfect union of yoghurt and pineapple weed, they are simple to put together and can be served warm or cold.

Ingredients

3–4 sheets filo pastry

25g/1oz butter, melted (or 1 tbsp sunflower oil)

2 free-range eggs

450g/1lb Greek yoghurt or curd cheese

150g/5oz Pineapple Weed Preserve (p.127)

Method

Preheat the oven to 200°C/180°C fan/400°F and grease a 12-hole muffin tin.

Cut the filo pastry into 36 squares, each 10x10cm/4x4in and cover the squares with a clean, damp tea towel until ready to use. Brush the middle of each square (not the edges) with a little butter (or oil), then lie 3 squares on top of each other, alternating the angle so they make a kind of star shape. It is easier to do this when the sheets are flat, then place the star into a muffin hole, gently pressing into the bottom and sides to make space for the filling. Continue with all the filo squares until all the muffin holes are filled.

Beat together the eggs and Greek yoghurt or curd cheese, then stir in the pineapple weed preserve and spoon equally into the pastry stars. Bake for 10–12 minutes or until the mixture is firm, then leave to cool before removing from the tin. These are best eaten fresh, but will keep in an airtight container for a couple of days.

131

Pineapple Weed and Coconut Ice Lollies

Makes 6 | Vegan and gluten-free

These lollies give a cooling hit of sweet, grassy pineapple weed, followed by a layer of puréed pineapple, sitting on a sweet coconut base. My niece and nephew, Fin and Elana, always devour them without a word – possibly the best feedback I could get! You'll need a lolly mould to make them; some have built-in sticks, but otherwise you can use traditional wooden ones.

Ingredients

100ml/3½fl oz Pineapple Weed Syrup (p.127)

200g/7oz canned or fresh pineapple, puréed in a blender or food processor

100ml/3½fl oz coconut milk

Method

Mix half the syrup with 100ml/3½fl oz water and pour into the lolly moulds so each is equally filled. Freeze for 2 hours.

Take out of the freezer and pour in the puréed pineapple to form the second layer, dividing the mixture equally between the moulds. If using wooden lolly sticks, the syrupy layer should be firm enough now to push a stick into each so the sticks stay upright. Freeze for a further hour.

Combine the remaining syrup with the coconut milk, stir well then top up each mould. If using lolly moulds that have built-in sticks on the lids, place the lids on now and return to the freezer. Eat within 1 month if using an unlidded lolly mould with wooden sticks, and within 6 months if using a lidded one.

Fennel Seeds

Foeniculum vulgare (Umbelliferae / Apiaceae)

With its aniseed taste and aroma, people tend to love or hate fennel; you can probably guess which camp I'm in. Fennel has been respected as a sacred herb since the Middle Ages – the seeds are a well-known soother for digestive problems and abdominal pain. High in vitamin C and a good source of fibre, potassium, calcium and phosphorous, they're often used to treat respiratory conditions, anaemia and are said to increase milk flow when breastfeeding. They can even solve bad breath – making fennel-infused desserts the perfect end to a meal.

Like hogweed (p.144), fennel is an umbellifer with umbrella-like flowerheads (which turn into seedheads). But fennel is easier to distinguish from its (sometimes poisonous) cousins, thanks to its strong scent and yellow flowers. Native to the Mediterranean and Southern Europe, it's been introduced to North Europe and much of North and South America, East Africa and West Asia. It is cultivated in many places across the world, and is even considered invasive in Australia and several areas of the US.

Main identifying features

Grows up to 2½m/8ft tall with long, hairless stems and fine, feathery leaves. Yellow flowerheads give way to narrow, aromatic seeds around ½–1cm/¼in long.

When to forage

Seeds start appearing in late summer and can be picked fresh or dried till mid to late autumn.

Where to forage

Favouring dry and well-drained soil, fennel prospers in coastal areas, wastelands and roadsides, and is also often planted in gardens.

How to forage

Cut the seedheads off at the stem and leave to dry before using, or pick the dry seeds individually while leaving the seedheads intact.

Cautions

The *umbelliferae* plant family includes some poisonous members so correct identification is paramount. Avoid fennel that may have been treated with pesticides in areas where it's considered invasive.

You can pick fennel when fresh and leave it to dry before collecting the seeds.

Fennel, Coconut and Yoghurt Slices

Makes 28–36

I love the combination of zingy fennel, sweet coconut and tart yoghurt in these bite-sized treats inspired by Egyptian *basbousa* (semolina cakes). They're satisfyingly substantial and have a gorgeous aniseed flavour.

Ingredients

1½ tsp fennel seeds

190g/7oz coarse semolina

45g/1¾oz desiccated coconut

35g/1¼oz rice flour

½ tsp baking powder

25g/1oz golden caster or granulated sugar

50g/2oz soft brown sugar

100g/3½oz thick natural yoghurt, at room temperature

100g/3½oz butter, melted and allowed to cool to room temperature

For the syrup

1 tsp fennel seeds

50g/2oz soft brown sugar

Method

Roughly grind all 2½ teaspoons of fennel seeds, either in a seed grinder or pestle and mortar, keeping some texture rather than making powder.

In a medium bowl, mix the semolina, coconut, flour, baking powder and golden caster or granulated sugar with the 50g/2oz soft brown sugar and 1½ teaspoons of fennel seeds, then add the yoghurt and melted butter and mix until well combined. The mixture should be quite stiff. Set aside for 1 hour to let the semolina absorb the rest of the ingredients.

Preheat the oven to 190°C/170°C fan/375°F and lightly grease a 20cm/8in square baking tray.

Press the mixture firmly and evenly into the baking tray. Cut into 6 strips lengthways, then into 6 diagonally to make diamond shapes. Bake for 25–30 minutes or until golden.

Meanwhile, make the syrup. Place the 50g/2oz soft brown sugar, 1 teaspoon of fennel seeds and 100ml/3½fl oz water in a small saucepan and bring to the boil, stirring until the sugar dissolves. Leave to simmer for 5 minutes, then remove from the heat and leave to cool.

As soon as you take the slices out of the oven, evenly pour over the syrup. Leave to cool in the tin completely before serving. Store in an airtight container for up to 1 week.

Fennel, Rose and Almond Milk Puddings

Serves 4 | Vegan and gluten-free

These puddings have the sumptuous texture of thick-set cream, even with no dairy in sight, and a delicate flavour of infused rose and fennel. I can happily eat one of these at any time of day. I use my homemade rose water (p.107), but you can use a shop-bought variety if you're pressed for time.

Ingredients

750ml/1⅓ pints unsweetened soya or other plant-based milk

50g/2oz golden granulated or caster sugar

50g/2oz cornflour

50g/2oz ground almonds or almond flour

1 heaped tsp fennel seeds, roughly ground

1 tsp homemade Rose Water (p.107) or ¼ tsp shop-bought rose water

To decorate (optional)

fresh or dried rose petals (see drying instructions on p.104)

ground fennel seeds

Method

In a small saucepan, warm one-third of the milk over a low heat until lukewarm, then remove from the heat and whisk in the sugar, cornflour and ground almonds or almond flour until the sugar has dissolved, then put aside.

Add the remaining milk to a medium saucepan with the ground fennel seeds and rose water and whisk until combined. Cook over a medium heat until almost boiling, then strain through a fine sieve or muslin cloth into a large bowl or jug, discarding the seeds. Pour the strained mixture immediately back into the medium saucepan.

Stir in the warm cornflour and milk mix and continue to whisk over a medium heat until the mixture starts to thicken. Remove from the heat and spoon into 4 small bowls or glasses. Leave to set for a couple of hours at room temperature. A skin will set on the top which you can peel off before serving, or leave. Serve chilled or at room temperature, decorated with some rose petals and ground fennel seeds, if you like.

Fennel and Gram Flour Biscuits

Makes 15 | Vegan

These sweet, compact biscuits have a surprisingly light quality and an Indian influence in their use of fennel and gram (chickpea) flour. Eat them with a mug of chai or your favourite tea, or serve them as an accompaniment to Fennel, Rose and Almond Milk Puddings (p.141).

Ingredients

1 heaped tbsp dried fennel seeds

125g/4½oz plain flour

25g/1oz wholemeal flour

75g/2¾oz unrefined icing sugar

1 heaped tbsp gram (chickpea) flour

75g/2¾oz olive oil

Method

Preheat the oven to 180°C/160°C fan/350°F and lightly grease a medium-sized baking tray.

Roughly grind the fennel seeds, either in a seed grinder or pestle and mortar, keeping some texture rather than making powder.

In a large bowl, combine all the dry ingredients, including the ground fennel seeds, before adding 2 tablespoons of water and the olive oil. Mix thoroughly – you may need to add a little more water to bind – then split the dough into 5 equal pieces.

Divide and roll each piece into 3 small balls, flattening to about 4–5cm/1½ –2in wide, to make 15 biscuits.

Bake for 20–25 minutes, or until they turn slightly golden at the edges, then remove from the oven and leave to cool on a cooling rack. Store in an airtight container for up to 1 week.

Hogweed Seeds

Heracleum sphondylium (Umbelliferae / Apiaceae)

Spicy, sweet, tingly and zesty, hogweed seeds taste a little like orange peel but somehow more floral. It's difficult to describe flavours we're not used to, and hogweed is just that: a fantastic, incomparable spice. I get excited about weeds, especially the unusual ones. In desserts, I usually pair these seeds with milder, warming ingredients such as pumpkin (as in my Pumpkin and Hogweed Seed Delights, p.148) to show off their aromatic, autumnal spiciness.

Native to Europe and Morocco and introduced to New Zealand, common hogweed (*Heracleum sphondylium*) is often misunderstood and presumed poisonous by humans. Although edible, it is considered a noxious weed in some parts of the world and comes with some important warnings. The sap of hogweed can cause blisters and scar if touched, especially on sunny days. Luckily, it's the dried seeds that are best as a spice, so you can avoid these green, sap-filled plants completely. Be sure to steer clear of giant hogweed (*Heracleum mantegazzianum*), too, which grows much larger than the common variety (3–5m/10–16ft tall with flowerheads up to 60cm/2ft wide) and is toxic. Picking dried hogweed in autumn, when it's grown to its full height, makes it easier not to be fooled by this giant, unwelcoming cousin.

Main identifying features

Grows 1–2m/3–7ft tall with umbrella-like seedheads up to 20cm/8in wide. The stems are hollow when dried and the seeds are flat, oval, tan-coloured discs, with two darker lines on the surface. Avoid fresh hogweed, when it has ridged, hairy stems, white flowerheads and serrated, hairy leaves – take note of the plant's location and come back in later months.

When to forage

Late summer through to early winter.

Where to forage

Wastelands, parks, the edges of woods, beside roads and railways, scrublands and in hedges.

How to forage

Pick off dried seeds individually. Alternatively, the dried seedheads can be cut at the stem and displayed in a vase as decorations (for up to 6 months) before you extract the seeds.

Cautions

Avoid when fresh and noxious – forage only when dried – and make sure to identify correctly, as many similar varieties are poisonous. Umbellifers are a large family that includes fantastic edibles, non-edibles and deadly poisonous plants, so correct identification is key. Make sure you are not picking or eating giant hogweed.

Other notable varieties

Cow parsnip (*Heracleum maximum*)

Hogweed should only be picked when dry: collect the distinctive seeds or snip off the seedheads to display.

Pumpkin and Hogweed Seed Delights

Makes 25

These soft and sweet delights have a distinct dark-sugar and hogweed-seed flavour and the pumpkin gives them a fantastic colour, too. They are both light and filling, making them a great snack or breakfast-on-the-go.

Ingredients

300g/10oz diced and peeled pumpkin or squash

250g/9oz plain flour

50g/2oz wholemeal flour

1 tsp baking powder

1 tsp bicarbonate of soda

1½ tbsp roughly chopped or ground hogweed seeds

½ tsp ground cinnamon (optional)

125g/4½oz butter, softened

125g/4½oz dark brown sugar

1 free-range egg

Method

Place the pumpkin or squash in a steamer basket over a saucepan of simmering water and steam for 15 minutes or until very soft, then mash and set aside to cool.

Preheat the oven to 180°C/160°C fan/350°F and grease two large, non-stick baking trays.

In a large bowl, combine the flours, baking powder, bicarbonate of soda, hogweed seeds and cinnamon, if using. In a separate bowl, cream together the butter and sugar, then add the mashed pumpkin or squash and beat in the egg until the mixture is creamy. Pour into the dry ingredients and stir to combine.

Using a tablespoon, drop large spoonfuls of mixture onto the baking tray, with space between them. Bake for 15–20 minutes until firm and leave to cool on the baking tray. Store in an airtight container and eat within 5 days.

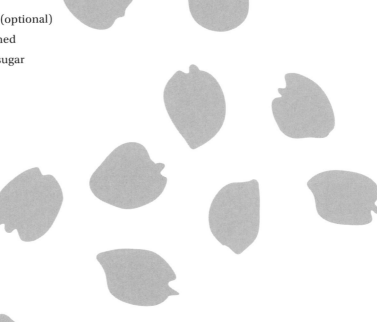

Sugared Hogweed Seeds and Almonds

Makes 300g/10oz | Vegan and gluten-free

These make a brilliant, crunchy, unrefined-sugar snack complete with the delightful zing of hogweed seeds. The recipe was inspired by my talented friend and collaborator, chef Fiona Were, who created a delicious hogweed-seed caramel for one of my foraging walks. I love the balance of protein-rich nuts with carbohydrate-laden sugars and, in my experience, these give a definite lift to sluggish afternoons.

Ingredients

1 heaped tbsp hogweed seeds

160g/5½oz golden granulated sugar

170g/6oz almonds, skins removed

Method

Roughly chop the hogweed seeds with a sharp knife on a chopping board or in a seed grinder. Line a large baking tray with baking parchment and, in a medium saucepan or frying pan, place the sugar, hogweed seeds and 45ml/1½fl oz water. Bring to the boil over a medium heat, then allow to reach 116°C/240°F on a sugar thermometer. Stir in the almonds. The mixture will naturally crystalise around the nuts. Continue cooking for about 15 minutes, letting the sugar liquify again and stirring regularly, until the almonds look lightly toasted and golden, and the sugar is a deep caramel colour, turning down the heat if it begins to burn.

Pour the mixture into the baking tray, spread out and leave to cool. Break up any large lumps of nuts and store in an airtight container. Will keep for up to 4 weeks in a cool, dark place.

Pear and Hogweed Seed Slice

Makes 9 squares
Can be made vegan and gluten-free

These moist and gooey squares of pear cake are spiced with hogweed seeds. My favourite version of this upside-down cake is a gluten-free, vegan recipe for extra stickiness, but if you prefer a firmer, spongier cake (pictured), use the eggs and plain flour in place of the aqua faba and gluten-free flour.

Ingredients

1½ tbsp dried hogweed seeds, ground

90g/3¼oz soft brown sugar, plus 1 level tbsp

200g/7oz pear (1 large pear), cored and cut into 1cm/½in slices

75ml/2½fl oz sunflower oil

3 tbsp apple juice

2 large free-range eggs (or 4 tbsp aqua faba – the liquid from a can of chickpeas)

100g/3½oz plain flour (or gluten-free flour), sifted

1 tbsp baking powder, sifted

¼ tsp bicarbonate of soda (if using aqua faba), sifted

Method

Preheat the oven to 200°C/180°C fan/400°F and line a 20cm/8in square cake tin with baking parchment.

Sprinkle half the ground hogweed seeds over the base of the tin, then sprinkle over the 1 tablespoon of sugar. Arrange the pear slices over the sugared and spiced base of the tin.

In a small bowl, beat the oil, apple juice, 90g/3¼oz sugar and eggs together. If using aqua faba, whizz the liquid in a food processor for 5 minutes or until it forms soft peaks (like egg whites) and put aside. Add the flour, baking powder and remaining ground hogweed seeds to a large bowl, plus the bicarbonate of soda if using the aqua faba. Stir to combine.

One-third at a time, pour the wet ingredients into the dry and stir to combine. Stir in the aqua faba last, if using, and combine well before pouring the mixture into the tin.

Bake for 25–30 minutes, or until a skewer comes out clean when pierced into the centre of the cake or the cake starts to come away from the sides. Allow to cool before slicing into squares. Keeps well for a few days in the fridge in an airtight container.

Cleaver Seeds

Galium aparine (Rubiaceae)

Cleavers are a hard plant to lose: they stick to the dog, the cat, your clothes and themselves. As children we called it 'sticky grass' and pretended to pat each other's backs while sticking stems to each other. As an adult, it was my caffeine-loving friend Chris who introduced me to the tiny, clingy seeds as the best wild substitute for coffee he knew, inspiring me to try baking my first cleaver-coffee cake.

A relation of the coffee plant, cleaver seeds do contain some caffeine and can act as a mild stimulant. When roasted, they release a gentle, warming, coffee-like flavour and scent ideal for drinks and desserts. Each plant can produce hundreds of seeds – anything from 300 to over 1,000 – giving you a huge bounty to forage if you have the patience. Native to Europe, much of Asia, the Middle East and North Africa, cleavers have been introduced across North America as well as in parts of South America, Australasia and Africa.

Main identifying features

Stems grow up to 3m/10ft long with thin, sticky leaves that die back when the seeds mature. White, inconspicuous flowers (just 1–2mm/⅛in across in summer) give way to seeds that are around 2mm/⅛in long and covered with tiny hooks.

When to forage

Late summer through to early winter when the seeds are hard and dry.

Where to forage

Fields, hedgerows and anywhere there's space for weeds to grow – from sea level up to around 450m/1,500ft.

How to forage

If you walk through a patch of cleavers several times in woolly clothes, this plant will pick itself for you – otherwise, collect handfuls of stems and rub them together over a container to collect the tiny seeds, or pick seeds individually with your fingers.

Cautions

The seeds are too hard to be eaten whole; don't try. Some people get a localised rash when in contact with fresh cleavers, but picking it when the stems and seeds are dry should avoid this.

Cleaver Coffee

Makes 100g/3½oz/6 tbsp
Vegan and gluten-free

For committed coffee drinkers, this wild substitute is the best invention I've found from the hedgerows. Though its subtle taste will underwhelm espresso drinkers, its coffee-like flavour suits desserts deliciously. This is the basis for all the drinks and edible treats in this section.

Ingredients

100g/3½oz cleaver seeds, picked off the stems, discarding as much stem as possible

Method

Preheat the oven to 180°C/160°C fan/350°F, place the seeds on a baking tray and dry roast for 45 minutes–1 hour. The more seeds you have, the longer the roasting will take. Let them darken until they smell a little of coffee, though don't let them burn.

Allow to cool, then store in a sealed, sterilised container at room temperature for up to 6 months. Grind on demand with a strong seed or coffee grinder. To make the coffee, add 2–4 tbsp ground cleaver grains to 250ml/8½fl oz water in a saucepan over a low heat, bring to the boil, simmer for 3 minutes, then strain.

Cleaver Coffee Custard Tartlets

Makes 12 | Can be made gluten-free

These tartlets are the perfect size to pop straight in your mouth. Set in a sweet, crisp pastry with an earthy-flavoured egg custard, their comforting sweetness helped me through several bitterly cold winter days when my heating was broken.

For the pastry

110g/4oz plain flour (or gluten-free flour)

55g/2oz cold butter, cubed, plus extra for greasing

1 tbsp soft brown sugar

2 tbsp cold Cleaver Coffee (p.157) or water

For the filling

2 tbsp ground Cleaver Coffee grains (p.157)

250ml/8½fl oz full-fat milk

2 free-range egg yolks

2 dessertspoons soft brown sugar

Method

To make the pastry, tip the flour into a mixing bowl and, using your fingertips, rub in the butter until the mixture resembles breadcrumbs. Stir through the soft brown sugar, then trickle in the cold coffee or water, and combine to make a wet dough. Wrap in baking parchment or a waxed food wrap and leave to sit in the fridge for 30 minutes.

Meanwhile, start making the filling. Place the cleaver coffee grains and milk in a small saucepan over a low heat, bring to the boil and simmer for 3 minutes. Then turn off the heat, cover and allow to slowly cool in the pan.

In a jug, whisk together the egg yolks and soft brown sugar until pale and fluffy. Once the milk has cooled to just lukewarm, strain it through a fine sieve into the jug with the egg and sugar mixture and whisk to combine.

Preheat the oven to 200°C/180°C fan/400°F and grease a 12-hole small tart tin (each hole should be 5–6cm/2in across and 1cm/½in deep).

Remove the dough from the fridge, break into 12 equal pieces then press 1 piece into each hole of the tin and shape with your fingers to create pastry cases. Make sure there are no gaps in the pastry. Pour in the filling, carefully transfer to the oven and bake for about 25 minutes. The tarts are ready when they slightly dome. Take out of the oven immediately and leave to cool before removing them from the tin. Store in an airtight container, and if not eating within the day, keep in the fridge for up to 5 days.

Cleaver Coffee Cupcakes

Makes 12

These cupcakes are decadently topped with a creamy cleaver-coffee icing and threaded through with fine grains of cleaver seeds, which give texture and flavour. Baking these reminds me of cake-making as a child; when an essential part of the process was my sisters and I accidently spilling lots of icing to dip our fingers into.

Ingredients

4 tbsp powdered Cleaver Coffee grains (p.157, but grind the seeds extremely finely, then sieve to make a powder)

150g/5oz butter

100g/3½oz soft brown sugar

40g/1½oz golden caster sugar

4 free-range eggs

150g/5oz self-raising flour (or 150g/5oz plain flour plus 2 tsp baking powder), sifted

For the topping

140g/4¾oz butter, softened

280g/9¾oz unrefined icing sugar, sifted

Method

Place the cleaver coffee grains with 200ml/6¾fl oz water in a small saucepan over a low heat, slowly bring to the boil and simmer for 3 minutes with the lid on. Take off the heat and leave to infuse and cool. Strain through a muslin cloth or fine sieve into a small bowl, squeezing out every drop of the cleaver liquid: there should be about 4 tablespoons. Put aside for later, and also put the used coffee grains aside for later.

Preheat the oven to 180°C/160°C fan/350°F and fill a 12-hole muffin tin with paper cases.

In a medium bowl, beat the 150g/5oz butter and the soft brown and golden caster sugars together, either by hand or with an electric whisk until light and fluffy. Add the eggs one at a time, beating each one in well. Add 2 tablespoons of the cleaver coffee and 1 tablespoon of the used coffee grains and stir well. Add the flour and combine thoroughly.

Spoon the mixture into the paper cases and bake for 18–20 minutes, or until the cakes are golden and a skewer inserted into the centre comes out clean. Leave to cool for 5 minutes before taking them out of the tin and leaving to cool completely on a cooling rack.

For the topping, add the butter to a medium bowl and beat until pale and fluffy. This is best done with an electric whisk to achieve a really light texture, but can be whisked by hand if needs be. Sieve in half the icing sugar and beat well to combine, then sieve in the remainder of the icing sugar and beat for a few minutes until you have a smooth, fluffy icing.

Add the remaining cleaver coffee and mix well. This will make a slightly runnier and glossier butter icing than usual, which can be firmed up in the fridge for 30 minutes, if needed, before using. You can use less liquid, but the flavour won't come through so well. Spoon the icing into a piping bag and use a nozzle to decorate the top of each cooled cake, or use a flat-edged knife to smother each cake top.

These keep well for a few days in an airtight container; keep in the fridge if using the runnier version of the butter icing.

Cleaver Coffee and Almond Semi-Freddo

Serves 8 | Gluten-free and dairy-free

This semi-freddo is a three-tiered heaven of cool, coffee-flavoured topping, creamy coconut middle and crunchy, nutty base. It's actually really easy to make – just remember each layer needs to firm up in the freezer before adding the next one. I like to let it melt a little before I dig in so it has a dreamy, soft texture.

Ingredients

4 tbsp ground Cleaver Coffee grains (p.157)

20g/¾oz unrefined icing sugar

2 x 400ml/13½fl oz cans coconut milk (must be suitable for whipping with no added stabilisers), chilled overnight

3 free-range egg yolks

60g/2¼oz soft brown sugar

25g/1oz ground almonds or almond flour

30g/1oz almonds, roughly chopped

coconut or vegetable oil, for greasing

Method

Lightly grease a 1-litre/1¾-pint lidded, freezer-proof container with coconut or vegetable oil. In a small saucepan, add the ground cleaver coffee grains and 400ml/13½fl oz water. Bring to the boil, cover and simmer for 2 minutes. Take off the heat and put aside to cool. Once cool, strain through a muslin cloth or fine-mesh sieve and put the liquid aside.

Place the icing sugar in a small bowl, measure out 100ml/3½fl oz the cleaver coffee you have just made and pour over the icing sugar. Whisk together, dissolving any lumps with the back of a spoon, before pouring into the loaf tin. Freeze for 1 hour; this will make the top layer.

For the second and third layers, open the coconut milk cans and weigh out 300g/10oz of the solid coconut pulp into a large bowl (the remaining coconut water can be used for drinks or curries). Add 4 tablespoons of cleaver coffee to the pulp and use an electric whisk to beat into a light, smooth cream that forms slight peaks. Put aside.

In a large bowl, add the egg yolks and the sugar and beat till lighter in colour and texture. Pour in the remaining cleaver coffee and the whipped coconut cream and mix well. Pour three-quarters of the mixture into the loaf tin, smooth over the top and freeze for a further 1 hour or until firm.

Stir the ground almonds or almond flour and chopped almonds into the remaining coconut cream mixture and smooth over the second layer of the semi-freddo. Cover and freeze for at least 2 hours: it will keep in the freezer for up to 1 month.

Remove from the freezer 15 minutes before serving and turn out onto a plate. You may need to slide a knife around the edges to loosen it out of the tin. Cut into slices to serve.

Autumn

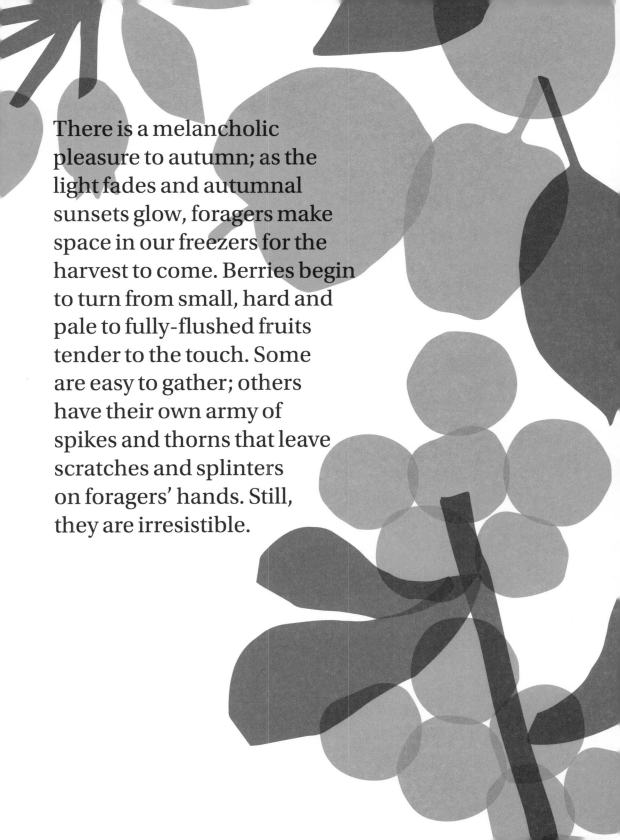

There is a melancholic
pleasure to autumn; as the
light fades and autumnal
sunsets glow, foragers make
space in our freezers for the
harvest to come. Berries begin
to turn from small, hard and
pale to fully-flushed fruits
tender to the touch. Some
are easy to gather; others
have their own army of
spikes and thorns that leave
scratches and splinters
on foragers' hands. Still,
they are irresistible.

Blackberries

Rubus fruticosus (Rosaceae)

'One for me, one for the pot' was the blackberry-picking rule I grew up with; each autumn, my family would head out armed with Tupperware to collect them from the patch of brambles across from our house. From sweet to sour, the flavour of blackberries varies immensely depending on the weather, time of year and the variety you're picking. Native to much of Europe and introduced in South Africa and South Korea as well as in parts of Australasia, many wild and cultivated varieties of blackberries thrive across the world.

In the UK, blackberries are our most foraged fruit; the tradition of going out blackberry picking brings together all ages (as do the pies and crumbles they're often turned into). Their small seeds are packed with omega 3 and 6 and plenty of fibre – so are worth taking time to chew. The fruits meanwhile are full of vitamins C and K with note-worthy amounts of B vitamins, potassium, magnesium, manganese and copper. Each variety produces a slightly different fruit; if you find a picking spot where they taste particularly delicious, it's worth remembering it to return to in future years. For, although the weather and soil influence their flavour, you may just have hit on the tastiest variety.

Main identifying features

Thorny stems that grow up to 4m/13ft long with white or pale pink five-petalled flowers and bulbous, purplish-black fruits that grow in clusters.

When to forage

Late summer through to mid-autumn – the earlier ones tend to be better raw, the later good for cooking.

Where to forage

Hedgerows, woodlands, scrublands and urban wastelands.

How to forage

Pick deep-black fruits (not the underripe red ones) that come away easily when pulled. They will temporarily stain your hands.

Cautions

Thorns can easily snag on skin and tear clothing. Blackberries are high in fibre and can cause a stomach upset if you eat too many (I speak from childhood experience).

Other notable varieties

Many other wild and cultivated varieties of blackberry (*Rubus*) grow across the world.

Blackberry Whisky

Makes 600ml/1 pint | Vegan and gluten-free

This is a very easy recipe: all that's required is whisky, blackberries and time. I blend it with Blackberry Cordial (below) to give a double berry hit. Drink slowly at whisky hour or use in my Blackberry Whisky and Chocolate Gateau (p.170).

Ingredients

500g/1lb 2oz blackberries

600ml/1 pint single malt whisky

Method

Place the blackberries in a sterilised jar or Kilner jar, pour over the whisky, place the lid tightly on and leave to mature for at least 3 weeks out of direct sunlight. Shake the jar every few days, or when you remember.

This will keep well for a couple of years. To serve, use a tea strainer, muslin cloth or fine sieve to strain off the blackberries (which can also be eaten) and add to a shot glass (along with 1 teaspoon of blackberry cordial, if you like!). Drink at room temperature or with ice: however you prefer your whisky.

Blackberry Cordial

Makes 350ml/11¾fl oz
Vegan and gluten-free

This blackberry cordial is divine; it has a deep, intense, fruity flavour. Use it in hot or cold drinks (dilute 1 part cordial with 5 parts water), drizzled over hot porridge, in Poached Pears and Blackberry Syrup Galettes (p.177) or to soak the sponges of a Blackberry Whisky and Chocolate Gateau (p.170).

Ingredients

500g/1lb 2oz blackberries

approx. 140g/4¾oz soft brown sugar

Method

Place the fruits in a medium saucepan with 1 tablespoon of water over a low–medium heat and mash a little with a wooden spoon. Cover and simmer for 10 minutes or until the fruits become soft and the pan is full of a simmering, dark liquid. Watch it doesn't bubble over.

Strain through a jelly bag, muslin or nylon cloth and leave to drip for at least 1 hour. You can squeeze the last drops out but be careful not to break the bag. You should have around 325ml/11fl oz liquid, but if you have significantly more or less you'll need to adjust the sugar quantity accordingly (4g/¼oz sugar for every extra 10ml/½fl oz).

Rinse the pan and return the liquid to it, then add the sugar and stir over a medium heat until the sugar has dissolved. Bring to the boil then remove from the heat and decant into a sterilised bottle. Store in the fridge for up to 6 months.

Blackberry Whisky and Chocolate Gateau

Serves 8–10 | Vegan

This gloriously moist, vegan chocolate cake is soaked with Blackberry Cordial and Whisky (p.169) and sandwiched together with Blackberry Preserve (p.172) and whipped coconut cream. It's decadent without being overly rich or sweet, making it practically impossible to stop at one slice.

For the sponge

1 tbsp ground chia or flax seeds

275g/9½oz self-raising flour (or 275g/9½oz plain flour plus 4 tsp baking powder)

75g/2¾oz light brown sugar

3 tbsp cocoa powder

1 tbsp baking powder

100ml/3½fl oz Blackberry Cordial (p.169) (optional, see Tip)

100ml/3½fl oz vegetable oil, plus extra for greasing

For the filling and topping

2 x 400ml/13½fl oz cans coconut milk (must be suitable for whipping with no added stabilisers), chilled overnight

1 dessertspoon golden granulated sugar (optional)

2 tbsp Blackberry Whisky (p.169) or water

2 tbsp Blackberry Cordial (p.169), plus extra for drizzling

175g/6oz Blackberry Preserve (p.172)

Method

Heat the oven to 180°C/160°C fan/350°F and grease two 20cm/8in cake tins.

Soak the ground seeds in 125ml/4¼fl oz water. In a large bowl, whisk together all the other dry sponge ingredients to remove any lumps, then add the soaked seeds and their water, the cordial and oil and whisk till smooth. Divide the mixture between the cake tins and spread with the back of a spoon until even. Bake for 25–30 minutes or until a skewer comes out clean. Leave to cool in the tins for 10 minutes, then carefully turn out onto a cooling rack – they're quite fragile, so be gentle.

Once the cakes are cool you can assemble with the fillings. Open the coconut milk cans and spoon out only the solid coconut cream at the top in to a bowl (put the coconut water aside to use in drinks or curries). Add the sugar, if using, and whip with an electric or hand whisk until creamy. Add a little of the coconut water, if too thick.

Place one of the cakes on a plate and, using a skewer, poke holes all over the surface. Mix the whisky or water and cordial in a jug and dribble half evenly over the cake. Next carefully spread the preserve across the cake (my blackberry preserve is quite thick, so I warm it in a small saucepan with 1 teaspoon of water first), followed by two-thirds of the whipped coconut cream. Place the second cake on top, again poking the surface all over, then dribble over most of the remaining cordial mixture and smother with the rest of the cream. When ready to serve, drizzle over the last of the cordial mixture, swirling into the cream in places, and leave to soak for at least an hour. Slice and enjoy. This cake keeps well in an airtight container in the fridge for up to 1 week.

Tip

You can omit the cordial in the sponge and instead use 100ml/3½fl oz water and double the sugar (150g/5oz), but the cake won't be as rich.

Blackberry Preserve

Makes 750g/1lb 10oz | Vegan and gluten-free

This is the best blackberry jam recipe
I know: rich with lots of texture and depth
from the whole blackberry fruits. It's gorgeous
lathered on toast, though I love it most as a
filling in Blackberry Whisky and Chocolate
Gateau (p.170).

Ingredients

500g/1lb 2oz blackberries

1 tbsp lemon juice

450g/1lb soft brown sugar

Method

In a medium saucepan, combine the
blackberries and lemon juice and simmer over
a medium heat for 10 minutes, mashing the
blackberries slightly with a wooden spoon to
break them up. Add the sugar, stirring regularly,
and bring to a rolling boil.

Once boiling, cook for 20 minutes without
stirring, or, if using a sugar thermometer, until
the mixture has reached 105°C/221°F and you
can do the setting test with it (see Tip). Pour or
spoon the jam into sterilised jars. Once opened,
keep in the fridge for up to 6 months.

Tip

To test if the preserve is ready and thick enough,
remove the pan from the heat, then take a
teaspoon of the mixture and drop it on to a clean,
chilled plate. Allow to cool for a few minutes
before pushing your finger or a spoon into the
edge of the preserve. If it begins to wrinkle at the
edges, it is ready. If it is too liquid, then return to
the heat and continue to simmer. Repeat the test
until ready.

Blackberry and Apple Curd

Makes 500g/1lb 2oz | Gluten-free

I've been known to greedily spoon this rich autumnal curd straight from the jar into my mouth. A balance of tart mingled with sweet, it's also a perfect filling for my Blackberry and Apple Curd Pie (p.174).

Ingredients

550g/1lb 4oz cooking or sour, wild apples, cores removed, chopped into small pieces

250g/9oz blackberries

2 tbsp cornflour

100g/3½oz soft brown sugar

85g/3oz butter, diced

3 free-range egg yolks

1 free-range egg

Method

Add the chopped apples, blackberries and 60ml/2fl oz water to a medium saucepan. Put the lid on and bring to the boil, then reduce the heat and simmer for 15 minutes or until the apples have gone soft. Don't let it cook for too long as you don't want to reduce the amount of liquid.

Take off the heat and strain through a jelly bag or muslin cloth, leaving to drip until you have 325ml/11fl oz juice. You may need to give the bag a gentle squeeze or two to get this amount. The leftover pulp can be stirred into porridge, muesli or mixed with yoghurt for breakfast.

Rinse out and dry the saucepan before adding the cornflour and sugar, mix well then slowly stir in the apple and blackberry juice to make a smooth paste. Place over a medium heat and stir constantly until thick, smooth and starting to bubble. Take off the heat and vigorously stir in the butter, allowing it to melt. Beat the yolks and egg together and pour into the pan. Return to a medium heat and keep stirring for 15–20 minutes, until the mixture thickens and reduces slightly, being careful not to let it burn on the bottom.

Pour into a sterilised jar and store in the fridge for up to 2 weeks.

Blackberry and Apple Curd Pie

Serves 8–10 | Gluten-free

This is no ordinary blackberry and apple pie. Made with a rich fruit curd and almond pastry, it has all the classic nostalgia of apples and blackberries but replaces cooked fruit with a lovely, thick, mousse-like centre. Savour every mouthful.

Ingredients

165g/5¾oz ground almonds

30g/1oz butter, melted

1 tbsp brown sugar

1 free-range egg, beaten

500g/1lb 2oz Blackberry and Apple Curd (p.173)

120g/4¼oz blackberries, to decorate (optional)

Method

Preheat the oven to 180°C/160°C fan/350°F and grease a 20cm/8in cake tin.

In a medium bowl, combine the ground almonds, melted butter, sugar and beaten egg and make into a ball. Using your fingers or the back of a metal spoon, press the mixture into the tin, aiming to get an even thickness, especially in the corners and up the sides.

Bake for 10 minutes before spooning in the curd and baking for a further 10 minutes. If the centre of the pastry has risen up, gently press it down before adding the curd.

Remove from the oven and place on a cooling rack for 30 minutes before removing from the tin. Leave to cool and set completely for at least another 30 minutes before sprinkling with blackberries, if using, then slice and serve. I find it is best to put it in the fridge for 30 minutes to help firm it up, and it will keep in the fridge in an airtight container for up to 3 days.

Poached Pears and Blackberry Syrup Galettes

Makes 12 | Gluten-free and dairy-free

Drenched in comforting Blackberry Cordial (p.169), these moreish buckwheat galettes make for a luxurious autumnal breakfast or substantial way to finish off a meal. They're also rather nice with the addition of homemade cashew nut cream (or dairy cream, if you prefer).

For the batter

330g/11¾oz buckwheat flour

pinch of sea salt

1 free-range egg, whisked

50ml/1¾fl oz vegetable oil (or 50g/2oz melted butter), plus extra for frying

For the filling

6 firm pears, peeled, cored and cut into 2cm/¾in chunks

400ml/13½fl oz Blackberry Cordial (p.169)

For the cashew cream

135g/4¾oz cashew nuts

1 tsp vanilla essence (optional)

1 tsp honey or golden granulated sugar (optional)

Method

To make the cashew cream, soak the cashews in water overnight. Drain, rinse and add to a blender with 150ml/5fl oz water, the vanilla and honey or sugar, if using. Blend to a smooth cream – if the texture is too thick, add a little water and blend again. It will keep for up to 5 days in the fridge in an airtight container.

To make the galette batter, mix the flour and salt in a large bowl before gradually adding 750ml/26fl oz water, about 250ml/8½fl oz at a time, and stirring in well. Beat in the egg and oil (or butter), then cover the batter and leave in the fridge for at least 30 minutes or overnight.

Place the pears in a medium pan with the cordial. Over a medium heat, simmer for 7–10 minutes, or until the pears are tender when pierced with a skewer or knife. Use a slotted spoon to lift out the pears and gently simmer the remaining juice for 30 minutes to reduce to 300ml/10fl oz syrup.

To cook the galettes, lightly grease a small to medium-sized frying pan with oil or butter (re-greasing between galettes if needed). Heat the pan over a medium heat and add 1 ladleful of batter, tipping the pan carefully in different directions to create an even, thin base of batter. Cook for about 2 minutes or until the galette starts to brown, then flip over and repeat on the other side. Keep warm on a plate with a clean tea towel over them, while you repeat until all the batter has been used. If making ahead of time, you can reheat the galettes in a dry frying pan, one at a time, to serve. They also freeze well once cooked and cooled (just place a piece of baking parchment between each one and store them in a sealed bag or an airtight, freezable container).

To serve, top each galette with some pear chunks and a dollop of cashew cream, then roll them up and drizzle over the cordial. Alternatively, serve in a stack, with the fillings piled on top.

Elderberries

Sambucus nigra (Caprifoliaceae)

It often seems to be raining when I collect elderberries. But autumnal downpours do make the berries sag lower on the tall elder tree, so they are at least a little easier to reach. Their deep, fruity flavour has a richness historically used to enhance wine or port, and brings a deep warmth to sweet treats. Worth getting drenched for, I think.

Elderberries, which are the fruits of the elder tree (from which elderflowers, p.84, can be picked earlier in the year), have been used for centuries as a remedy for coughs and colds, and can help relieve symptoms of bronchitis and similar conditions. Native to Europe, the common elder tree has also been introduced in areas of Australasia, South America and North Africa. Abundant in vitamins A and C, they're ideal for preventing winter sniffles (another reason to brave the rain to gather them), and were used for their medicinal qualities long before vitamin C-rich oranges and lemons came to British shores. The picking season is short for these fruits, so start to look out for them as soon as autumn arrives.

Main identifying features

Elder trees grow up to 6m/20ft tall with knobbly, cork-like trunks and branches and dull green, long, serrated and pointed leaves that grow opposite each other with one at the tip. Clusters of small, dark berries hang loosely, each fruit about 5mm/⅛in across.

When to forage

Early autumn.

Where to forage

Wastelands, parks, the edges of woods, roadsides, beside railways, scrublands and in hedges.

How to forage

Pick the clusters of berries by hand (the berries will stain your hands temporarily) or with scissors, then use a fork to detach the individual fruits at home.

Cautions

The leaves and stems have a mild toxicity and shouldn't be eaten, while the raw berries can cause stomach upsets.

Other notable varieties

Pink elder (*Sambucus nigra, f. porphyrophylla*)
American black elderberry (*Sambucus canadensis*)

Elderberry Cordial

Makes approx. 450ml/¾ pint
Vegan and gluten-free

A rich, non-alcoholic liquor with warming spices, I find this cordial divinely comforting sipped neat on cold evenings or used in any of the desserts in this section.

Ingredients

500g/1lb 2oz elderberries, stalks removed

10–15 cloves

2cm/¾in piece of fresh ginger, roughly chopped

1–2 cinnamon sticks

4 star anise

350g/12oz dark brown sugar

Method

Place the berries in a medium saucepan and add enough water to just cover them. Crush the berries with the back of a wooden spoon, add the spices and bring to the boil, simmering with a lid on for 20 minutes.

Pour the mixture through a sieve, mashing to ensure you extract all the juice. Clean the pan and return the sieved elderberry juice to the pan, adding the sugar. Place over a medium heat and stir while the sugar dissolves, then simmer for 10 minutes before allowing to cool and storing in a sterilised bottle. Keeps for 6 months in the fridge.

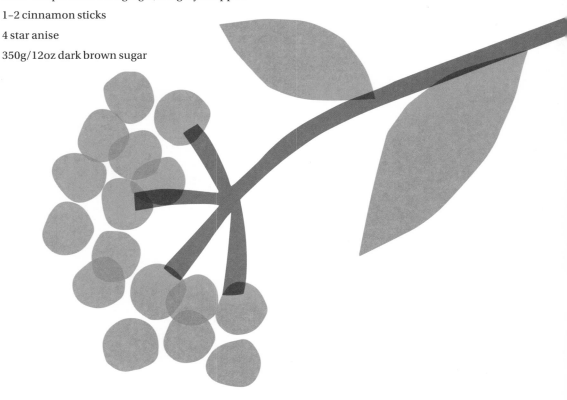

Elderberry and Apple Fruit Pastilles

Makes 25 | Vegan and gluten-free

Imagine making the perfect fruit pastille: tart, fruity and juicy. Well, imagine no more – this recipe hits the mark with both flavour and texture, and is naturally set by the fruits and unrefined sugar. They're good for coughs and chesty colds due to the berries' antiviral properties, too.

Ingredients

400g/14oz apples, roughly chopped (cores and all)

150g/5oz elderberries

400g/14oz golden granulated sugar

1 tbsp lemon juice

100ml/3½fl oz Elderberry Cordial (p.181)

50g/2oz demerara sugar, for coating (optional)

Method

Line a 20cm/8in square tin with baking parchment.

Place the chopped apples and the elderberries in a medium, heavy-based pan and add 250ml/8½fl oz water. Bring to the boil, cover and cook over a medium heat for about 20 minutes until soft and mushy. Strain the fruit through a fine sieve or muslin cloth, until you've extracted around 350ml/11¾fl oz juice. Rinse the pan and return the liquid to it along with the golden granulated sugar, lemon juice and elderberry cordial. Cook over a low heat, stirring until the sugar has dissolved, then turn up the heat and bring to the boil.

Reduce the heat to medium and simmer for 30 minutes, then raise the heat so the mixture reaches a rolling boil and let it thicken nicely and reach 112°C/234°F on a sugar thermometer. Watch the temperature, thickness and aroma really carefully, because it can burn easily at this point. When it reaches the right temperature, or there's a first whiff of burning, immediately take it off the heat and pour into the tin. Leave to cool.

Keep in the fridge in an airtight container for up to 1 month. Cut in to squares as needed, using a knife heated in hot water for ease, then roll the squares in demerara sugar, if you wish. The pastilles can also be rolled into different shapes in your hands.

Elderberry and Chocolate Soufflés

Makes 4 | Gluten-free and dairy-free

'Oh my God' is the standard response to the first mouthful of one of these soufflés. Everyone knows that chocolate tastes good, but the additional richness of Elderberry Cordial (p.181) in these light, fluffy, warm desserts makes them utterly irresistible.

Ingredients

50g/2oz vegan dark chocolate (minimum 70% cocoa solids), broken into small pieces

2 tbsp cornflour

150ml/5fl oz Elderberry Cordial (p.181)

2 free-range eggs, separated

1 free-range egg white

Method

Preheat the oven to 190°C/170°C fan/375°F.

Add the chocolate, cornflour and elderberry cordial to a small saucepan and heat over a low heat until the chocolate has melted. Increase the heat a little and stir until the mixture thickens, then put aside to cool slightly.

Meanwhile, in a spotlessly clean bowl, whisk all 3 egg whites until they form soft peaks, then mix the egg yolks into the elderberry and chocolate sauce. Spoon one-third of the egg whites into the sauce and combine, before softly folding in the rest.

Pour into four ramekins or oven-proof espresso cups and bake for 12 minutes or until the soufflés have risen sufficiently. Don't be tempted to open the oven prematurely as this makes them deflate. Serve immediately as a standalone dessert.

Elderberry and Vanilla Sponges

Makes 5

Crispy-edged individual sponges, still warm from the oven and topped with a generous soaking of Elderberry Cordial (p.181): what's not to love? These cakes are a lovely way to end a meal, leaving you with a cosy feeling inside. You can prepare the cake mixture beforehand and just pop them in the oven 30 minutes before you're ready for dessert.

Ingredients

150g/5oz butter, softened

125g/4½oz golden caster sugar

2 large free-range eggs, beaten

25g/1oz ground hazelnuts or almonds

75g/2¾oz self-raising flour (or 75g/2¾oz plain flour plus 1 tsp baking powder)

1 tsp baking powder

1 tsp vanilla extract

100ml/3½fl oz Elderberry Cordial (p.181)

crème fraîche, to serve (optional)

Method

Preheat the oven to 180°C/160°C fan/350°F and grease five individual pudding bowls or ramekins.

In a large mixing bowl, beat together the butter and sugar until pale and fluffy. Add the eggs, ground nuts, flour, baking powder and vanilla extract and beat well until combined.

Spoon the mixture into the bowls or ramekins and bake for 25 minutes or until risen and golden on top. Remove from the oven and leave to stand for 10 minutes.

If the middles have domed you may need to slice the tops off so the sponges each have a flat base. Tip out onto small plates, prick the tops with a skewer and spoon some elderberry cordial over each of them. Serve immediately just as they are or with crème fraîche.

Sloes

Prunus spinosa (Rosaceae)

Concealed within the dark, almost black, spiny branches of the blackthorn, sloes are a crafty fruit that are sometimes hard to spot. The smallest member of the plum family, I often dare people to try one raw – their tartness and the way they dry out your cheeks is quite unique and only needs to be experienced once! When cooked, however, they add an enticing fruitiness to desserts. Sloes are mostly known for the warming, sweet flavour they can give to gin, but be not mistaken; there's plenty more to these little berries than that.

Native to Europe, West Asia and some parts of North Africa, blackthorn has been introduced in Tasmania and areas of North America. Its berries are known for settling digestive upsets and have antibacterial and anti-inflammatory properties, making them beneficial for many ailments. The fruits contain vitamins C and E and magnesium, as well as traces of multiple other vitamins and minerals.

Main identifying features

Blackthorn grows up to 5m/16ft tall as a shrub or a small tree, with dark, spiky branches and small, serrated leaves. The berries are perfectly round, black or dulled purple and around 1–1½cm/½in across.

When to forage

Early to mid-autumn.

Where to forage

Woodlands, hedges, along riverbanks, scrublands, rocky places, waysides, steep slopes, dry coppices and meadows.

How to forage

Best picked with gloved hands to avoid the thorns and after the first frost when the fruits tend to be softer and sweeter. You can also pick them earlier and freeze them to 'fake' this stage.

Cautions

Cuts from the blackthorn have a reputation for going septic, especially if that long, tough thorn breaks off under the skin, so pick with care.

Sloe Gin

Makes 1¼ litres/2¼ pints (with fruits),
or 850ml/1½ pints strained
Vegan and gluten-free

Warming, spicy and complex with a deep hue of red, this sloe gin is simple to make and far superior to the shop-bought version. I love to sip it neat or add a splash or two to my decadent Sloe Gin Chocolate Cake (p.192).

Ingredients

1 x 750ml/26fl oz bottle of gin

300g/10oz sloes picked after first frost, defrosted if frozen

200g/7oz golden granulated sugar

Method

Pour the gin into a jug and half-fill the bottle it came out of with sloes. Using a funnel or a jug with a spout, pour in just enough of the sugar to cover the fruits, then pour the gin back in until the bottle is full. Repeat with a second empty, sterilised, sealable bottle to use any remaining fruits and alcohol.

Screw the tops on and store in an accessible place, out of direct sunlight, where you can regularly shake the bottles to help release the colour and flavour. Leave for at least 3 months before drinking. You can leave the fruits in to let the flavour mature indefinitely or until you are happy with the taste. When ready, strain through a muslin cloth or fine sieve into a large bowl and rebottle.

Sloe Syrup

Makes approx. 600ml/1 pint
Vegan and gluten-free

This thick, rich syrup has a flavour reminiscent of tart plums and a slightly dry aftertaste. When diluted as a drink or poured over porridge, it's something of an acquired taste, but in my Sloe Treacle Tart (p.197) it adds only a wonderfully wild, fruity flavour: a guaranteed crowd-pleaser.

Ingredients

750g/1lb 10oz sloes

600g/1lb 5oz dark muscovado sugar

Method

Put the sloes, sugar and 325ml/11fl oz water in a medium saucepan, bring to the boil, then lower the heat a little until still bubbling but not a rolling boil. Cook uncovered for 45 minutes.

Take off the heat and leave to cool a little before straining through a colander, sieve, jelly bag or muslin cloth, pressing the fruits slightly to extract the last of the syrup. Store in a sterilised bottle in the fridge for up to 6 months.

Tip

The remaining fruits can be pitted and kept for the Sticky Sloe and Nut Clusters on p.194. This recipe creates about 200–300g/7–10oz sticky sloes. The amount depends on how thoroughly you remove all the sticky flesh from the stones.

Sloe Gin Chocolate Cake

Serves 8–10 | Can be made gluten-free

An indulgent combination of rich, gin-soaked sloes and dark chocolate means every mouthful of this boozy, moist cake is to be savoured. Low in flour and high in chocolate, it's the kind of dessert that conjures up the phrase 'death by chocolate' – in a good way.

Ingredients

300g/10oz gin-soaked sloes, pitted (see Tip)

4–5 tbsp Sloe Gin (p.191; if using gluten-free flour, use 5 tbsp), plus extra for serving (optional)

160g/5½oz dark chocolate (minimum 70% cocoa solids)

2–3 tbsp boiling water (3 if using gluten-free flour)

160g/5½oz butter, cut into small cubes

110g/4oz plain, rice or gluten-free flour, sifted

1 tsp baking powder, sifted

2 tbsp cocoa powder, sifted, plus extra for dusting

100g/3½oz soft brown sugar

4 free-range eggs, separated

Method

Preheat the oven to 190°C/170°C fan/375°F. Grease and line a 20cm/8in cake tin with baking parchment.

Put aside about 30 good-shaped halves of the pitted sloes for decoration. Place the rest in a food processor with the sloe gin and blend until roughly puréed.

Place a heatproof bowl over a saucepan of simmering water (the bowl should not touch the water). Break the chocolate into the bowl and leave to melt before stirring in the boiling water. Add the butter to the chocolate, leaving it to soften, then stir and take off the heat.

Meanwhile, in a large bowl, mix the flour, baking powder, cocoa and sugar together and set aside.

In a separate bowl, whisk the egg yolks until frothy, then stir them into the (slightly cooled) chocolate and butter mix. Fold in the sloe purée.

In a large, spotlessly clean bowl, whisk the egg whites until stiff peaks form. Pour the chocolate mix, then the egg whites, into the dry ingredients and gently fold in until the mixture is thoroughly combined but not beaten.

Pour the mixture into the cake tin and bake for 40 minutes, or until a skewer inserted into the centre of the cake comes out clean. Allow to cool in the tin for 10 minutes before turning out onto a cooling rack. Decorate with the reserved sloes and, using a sieve, dust lightly with cocoa powder. Store in an airtight container for up to 5 days – and serve soaked with an extra splash of gin, if you want a truly boozy dessert.

Tip

You can use the gin-soaked sloes left over from making Sloe Gin (p.191) in this recipe. Stone the sloes by squashing them between your fingers, or against a chopping board, trying to remove as much of the flesh as possible.

Sticky Sloe and Nut Clusters

Makes 36 | Vegan

These scrummy snacks are gooey, sweet, sticky, crunchy, and hard not to finish in one sitting. The leftover fruits from making Sloe Syrup (p.191) are perfect used up in this vegan, moreish recipe.

Ingredients

40ml/1¼fl oz rapeseed oil

140g/4¾oz demerara or soft brown sugar

200g/7oz sticky sloes, pitted (see Tip)

70g/2½oz plain flour

1 heaped tsp cornflour

150g/5oz almonds or hazelnuts, roughly chopped

Method

Preheat the oven to 200°C/180°C fan/400°F. Line a large baking tray (30x40cm/12x16in) or two smaller ones with baking parchment.

In a medium bowl, combine the oil and sugar, add 1 teaspoon of water and the sticky sloes, stir, then add the flour, cornflour and nuts. Stir well to create an even mixture.

Make the clusters by distributing heaped teaspoons of the mixture evenly across the baking trays, with enough space between them for the mixture to spread a little.

Bake for approximately 12 minutes, or until the clusters are bubbling and dark brown at the edges. Remove from the oven immediately and leave for 5 minutes before gently removing from the tray and onto a cooling rack. Store in an airtight container at room temperature and enjoy within 1 week.

Tip

Use the sloes from making Sloe Syrup (p.191) and take your time to remove and discard the stones so you can keep as much flesh as possible. I take around 20–30 minutes to get 200g/7oz sticky sloes.

Sloe Treacle Tart

Serves 8–10

This dark, rich and wonderfully fruity treacle tart is a hearty treat for colder months with a beautifully crumbly oatmeal pastry. I love to indulge in a slice as an afternoon snack.

Ingredients

90g/3¼oz plain flour, plus extra for dusting

90g/3¼oz wholemeal flour

2 tbsp soft brown sugar (optional)

50g/2oz oatmeal

125g/4½oz butter, cut into cubes

2–3 tbsp ice-cold water

400ml/13½fl oz Sloe Syrup (p.191), plus 2 tbsp

75g/2¾oz oats

75g/2¾oz fresh breadcrumbs (made from fresh bread, grated or food-processed)

2 free-range eggs

Method

In a large bowl, mix the flours, sugar and oatmeal together, then add the butter. Rub the mixture together using your fingertips or tip into a food processor and blitz until thoroughly combined and resembling fine breadcrumbs. Add the cold water, one tablespoon at a time, combining after each tablespoon until it comes together into a dough (you may not need all the water). Place in a bowl, tightly cover with baking parchment or a waxed food wrap, then refrigerate for 30 minutes.

Meanwhile, preheat the oven to 180°C/160°C fan/350°F and grease a 23cm/9in flan tin.

Take the pastry out of the fridge and roll out on a lightly floured surface, until it's large enough to fill the tin and line the sides. Mine often falls apart at this stage, don't worry, just press it back together. Carefully lift the pastry into the tin, gently pressing into the corners and slicing off any excess. Pop the tin in the fridge to firm up for 10 minutes or more, then line with baking parchment and baking beans or uncooked rice. Bake in the oven for 15 minutes.

While the pastry is baking, gently heat the sloe syrup in a small saucepan, until lukewarm. Stir in the oats and breadcrumbs, then put aside.

Take the pastry case out of the oven and reduce the temperature to 150°C/130°C fan/300°F. Remove the parchment and beans or rice.

Whisk the eggs in a bowl and pour into the heated syrup mix, stirring until combined well, then pour the filling into the pastry base. Bake for 35 minutes or until set.

Take out of the oven and spoon over the 2 tablespoons of sloe syrup, then leave to cool in the tin on a cooling rack before carefully removing from the tin. Serve warm or cold. This keeps well in the fridge for up to 1 week.

Crab Apples

Malus sylvestris (Rosaceae)

Wild apples are a lottery to bite into; there's no knowing if they will taste floral, sharp or decidedly sour. Crab apples are some of my favourites for their wonderful tartness that combines beautifully with sugar to make complex sweets. Crab apple trees can live up to 100 years old. Occasionally I find a truly wild one in a woodland, but many cultivated varieties appear in gardens or on tree-lined streets, where their tiny apples roll across the pavement. These types are equally delicious – just not as sharp as the original, wild crab apple.

I was brought up with that old Welsh saying, 'an apple a day keeps the doctor away'; indeed, crab apples are packed with antioxidants, vitamins and fibre. Apples have been around since prehistoric times and there are now over 6,000 cultivated varieties worldwide, all originating from wild apples. Crab apples are native to Europe and Turkey, but have been introduced in north-east Australia and southern Argentina.

Main identifying features

The crab apple tree grows up to 12m/40ft tall with simple, serrated leaves and red or yellow fruits (around 2–3cm/1in across) with one to two small seeds in the centre. The UK's native, wild crab apples are round and yellow when ripe, but another common variety here is slightly larger (though still small) and more apple-shaped. Cultivated varieties (as pictured here) are small and yellowy-red to fully red.

When to forage

Early to late autumn.

Where to forage

Mature woodlands, hedgerows, wastelands, scrublands, grass verges, gardens and urban streets.

How to forage

To pick crab apples, twist the stem: if they come away easily, they are ripe.

Crab Apple Tarte Tatin

Serves 8

This stunning tart with caramelised apples and melt-in-the-mouth cinnamon pastry is a perfect dessert for autumn evenings. It's a little fiddly to make, but well worth the effort – and you only need to use one pan.

For the pastry

150g/5oz plain flour

20g/¾oz wholemeal flour

30g/1oz ground almonds

110g/4oz cold butter, diced

1 heaped tsp ground cinnamon

1 free-range egg, whisked

For the topping

350g/12oz crab apples

85g/3oz golden caster sugar

60g/2¼oz cold butter, plus 20g/¾oz, melted

Method

First make the pastry by combining the flours, ground almonds, diced butter and cinnamon in a food processor, or place in a bowl and rub together with your fingertips, until you achieve a fine breadcrumb texture. Add the egg and bring together into a ball of dough. Place in a bowl tightly covered with baking parchment or a waxed food wrap and refrigerate for 30 minutes.

Preheat the oven to 190°C/170°C fan/375°F.

Cut the crab apples in half and scoop out the centre of the apple (seeds and seed case), discarding any bruised ones. I do this using a sharp knife, not digging too deep.

You'll need a 25cm/10in ovenproof frying pan. Over a medium heat, sprinkle the sugar evenly into the pan, then slice the cold butter for the topping and place evenly across the sugar. Leave until it bubbles and browns slightly. Do not stir, though you can tip the pan to help the mixture melt.

Take off the heat and place the crab apples in the pan, curved side down and cut side up. Pack the apples tightly together, starting around the outside and working towards the centre.

Remove the pastry from the fridge, leave to sit for 10 minutes, then bang the dough ball a couple of times in each direction with a rolling pin before rolling it, to stop it from cracking. Roll out the pastry on a lightly floured surface to about 30cm/12in across.

Brush the cut edges of the apples in the pan with the melted butter. Place the pastry over the apples, tucking the overflow of pastry into the edges of the pan and cutting off any corners. Make about 6 small cuts evenly spaced into the pastry (to help steam escape) and bake in the oven for 20–25 minutes or until the pastry is golden and the apple juices are bubbling at the corners. While still warm, turn the tart out onto a plate, pastry side down. Serve warm or cold and enjoy within 24 hours to experience it at its best.

Crab Apple Jelly

Makes 325g/11½oz | Vegan and gluten-free

Traditional British jellies and jams are often high in refined sugar, but this recipe uses 20% less sugar and only unrefined golden rather than refined white. It has a fantastic flavour, texture and colour and is really very simple to make. Try using it in my Chocolate Crab Apple Jelly Cakes (p.206).

Ingredients

250g/9oz crab apples, roughly chopped

approx. 200g/7oz golden granulated sugar

Method

Place the apples in a medium saucepan and add enough water to cover them. Bring to the boil, turn down the heat, place a lid on and simmer for 30 minutes, mashing the fruits occasionally with a fork or wooden spoon.

Using a jelly bag or muslin cloth, strain the fruits into a bowl or measuring jug, allowing the juice to drip through. Suspend the cloth or bag above the container (tie above or fit to the container with a strong elastic bag) and leave to strain for a couple of hours or overnight.

Discard the fruits and measure out the juice. Pour into a medium saucepan and add 15g/½oz sugar for every 25ml/¾fl oz juice (60g/2¼oz sugar to every 100ml/3½fl oz juice). Bring to a gentle simmer, stirring to dissolve the sugar, then bring to a rolling boil for 10–15 minutes until the temperature reaches 105°C/221°F on a sugar thermometer (or it passes the setting test: see Tip on p.172). The jelly sets very quickly, so once off the heat pour immediately into sterilised jars and seal. Keeps for up to 6 months in the fridge.

Candied Crab Apples

Serves 4–6 | Gluten-free and dairy-free

In this recipe, crab apples are turned into a pretty, candied treat that few can resist. These sweets take seven days to create, but they last for weeks and are great with drinks, on their own or served with a cheese board. (These are pictured, in the bowl, on p.205.)

Ingredients

250g/9oz crab apples

240g/8¾oz golden caster sugar

1 tbsp honey

Method

Wash the apples and, using a needle, prick each 2–3 times in different places. Place them in a medium pan and cover with boiling water, or until the pan is half full as the apples will bob to the surface. Bring to the boil and immediately take the pan off the heat. Leave for 10 minutes before straining the liquid from the pan into a measuring jug, then decant the apples into a large, heatproof bowl.

To make the syrup, add 125g/4½oz of the sugar, the honey and 225ml/8fl oz reserved cooking liquid back into the saucepan. Slowly bring to the boil, over a low heat, stirring to dissolve the sugar, then simmer for 3 minutes or until you have a clear, syrupy mixture. Pour the syrup over the apples, stirring gently to coat them, then cover and put aside for 24 hours.

The following day, strain the syrup (reserving the apples) and pour it into a small saucepan. Add 25g/1oz sugar and bring to the boil, then take off the heat and tip the apples back in. Cover and leave for a further day.

Repeat this process each day for another 2 days, then on the fifth day (the first day was starting the process, plus 3 days adding to the syrup) add 40g/1½oz sugar, plus the syrup and fruits to a medium saucepan and simmer for 3 minutes. Pour the contents back into the heatproof bowl, cover and leave for 48 hours.

After a week – yes, that's all the hours added up so far – remove the fruits (see Tip) with a slotted spoon and leave to dry in a warm, dry place – near a radiator or in an oven set to the lowest temperature (no warmer than 50°C/120°F) on a cooling rack. Turn the fruits regularly to ensure they dry on all sides. Store, layered with baking parchment, in an airtight container for up to 2 weeks.

Tip

Once you remove the fruits, you'll find that you have a lot of crab-apple flavoured syrup left. This is perfect for glazing the Glazed Apple and Date Rock Cakes on p.204.

Glazed Apple and Date Rock Cakes

Makes 12 | Dairy-free

You can't go wrong with rock cakes; these moist bites of soft sponge enclosing chunks of apple and date are simply delightful. They're flavoured and glazed with the leftover syrup from making Candied Crab Apples (p.203) to give them a wild, sweet lift.

Ingredients

260g/9¼oz self-raising flour (or 260g/9¼oz plain flour plus 3 tsp baking powder)

85g/3oz wholemeal flour

1 level tsp bicarbonate of soda

1 level tsp baking powder

1 tsp ground chia seeds

425g/15oz apples (approx. 3 medium apples), cored and chopped into small chunks

125g/4½oz chopped dates

225ml/8fl oz soya milk or other plant-based milk

75ml/2½fl oz vegetable oil

200ml/6¾fl oz crab apple syrup (leftover from making the Candied Crab Apples on p.203)

Method

Preheat the oven to 190°C/170°C fan/375°F and lightly grease a 12-hole muffin tin with oil.

Mix together the dry ingredients in a large bowl. Add the apples and the dates and stir until the fruits are covered in the dry mixture. Pour in the milk, oil and 75ml/2½fl oz of the crab apple syrup and combine well with a wooden spoon. Spoon a generous amount of mixture into each muffin hole and bake for 25 minutes or until golden.

Once baked, prick each cake a few times with a skewer then drizzle 1 teaspoon of the crab apple syrup over each cake. Use a spoon or knife to tease out each cake from the tin and place on a cooling rack. Drizzle over the remaining glaze and leave to cool. Store in a sealed container for up to 1 week in the fridge and enjoy for breakfast or as snacks.

Chocolate Crab Apple Jelly Cakes

Makes 15 | Dairy-free

These were inspired by the gorgeous tart flavour of crab apples and childhood memories of Jaffa Cakes. These wild versions are sandwiched with flavourful Crab Apple Jelly (p.202), and they're quick and easy to make. My friend Sara and I once secretly enjoyed them in the cinema, and they did seem to help energise our walk home.

Ingredients

2 large free-range eggs

50g/2oz golden caster sugar

60g/2¼oz plain flour

150g/5¼oz Crab Apple Jelly (p.202)

150g/5¼oz vegan dark chocolate (minimum 70% cocoa solids), broken into pieces

Method

Preheat the oven to 180°C/160°C fan/350°F and lightly grease 15 holes of two 12-hole small tart tins (each hole should be 5–6cm/2in across and 1cm/½in deep).

Place a heatproof bowl over a small saucepan of simmering water. Do not let the water touch the bowl. Add the eggs and sugar into the bowl and whisk for about 5 minutes, or until they are pale and frothed up. Take off the heat and whisk in the flour, combining really well. Spoon into the tart tin and bake for 8–10 minutes, or until golden on top and a skewer comes out clean when poked into the centres. Take out of the oven and leave for 5 minutes before turning out onto a cooling rack to cool completely.

Once cooled, spoon 1 heaped teaspoon of crab apple jelly on the top of each cake, evening it out slightly.

Next, melt the chocolate. Place in a heatproof bowl over a small saucepan of simmering water, just like you did with the cake mixture. Once the chocolate is half melted, using a teaspoon, start to spoon it over the tops of the jelly on the cakes. Turn off the heat – the chocolate will continue to melt, but this will stop it over-heating and going grainy while you coat the rest of the jelly cakes. Let the chocolate harden for a couple of hours, then store in an airtight container and eat within a few days.

Rosehips

Rosa canina (Rosaceae)

Distinctively shaped, the bright red hips of the rose always catch my eye. Back in the summer the plant's petals can be gathered (p.104), but in autumn its fruits – known as hips – begin to ripen. All roses produce hips, but not all are tasty. My favourites, for their fruity, tart flavour, are the slender, oval fruits of dog roses (*Rosa canina,* pictured right), which are native to Europe and have been introduced in North America and parts of South America and Australasia. I also often use field roses (*Rosa arvensis*) and, nearer the coast, the big, fleshy Japanese rosehips (*Rosa rugosa,* pictured on p.105) are delicious, too – this variety was originally planted in the UK to stabilise sand dunes and shingle beaches.

Rosehips contain a tight ball of pesky, irritating seeds, so they are tricky, but not impossible to eat raw – I use my front teeth to nibble at the flesh of larger hips, stopping before I get to the seeds. Smaller hips are fiddlier still, and are best used for Rosehip Syrup (p.211), where you can sieve out the seeds. Despite these difficulties, rosehips are worth persevering with. They are bursting with vitamins A, C, K and B and can help stave off colds and flu through the frostier months – roll on winter, we foragers are prepared.

Main identifying features

Roses grow up to 1½m/5ft tall with thorny stems. Hips are red to orangey-red (deepening to a fuller red when ripe), oval and around 2–4cm/¾–1½in long.

When to forage

Early autumn to early winter.

Where to forage

Wastelands, hedges, parks, the edges of woods, roadsides, beside railways, scrublands and in gardens.

How to forage

Pick the hips when they are fully flushed red and slightly soft to the touch. They are best picked after the first frost, though you can freeze them to 'fake' this stage.

Cautions

Don't eat hips whole: the hairs covering their seeds can irritate the skin and digestive system.

Other notable varieties

Japanese rose (*Rosa rugosa*)
Field rose (*Rosa arvensis*)
As well as wild rosehips, you can also use many cultivated varieties of the *Rosa* species.

Rosehip Syrup

Makes 750ml/1⅓ pints
Vegan and gluten-free

This mildly fruity syrup is like a comforting tonic for the throat; it makes my tongue tingle and is brilliant at staving off colds. Dilute 1 part syrup to 5 parts water for drinks or use in the topping for Glazed Rye and Rosehip Biscuits (p.212). You lose very little of the vitamin C by infusing the rosehips this way – and most of that is lost in the time between mashing the fruits and cooking them, so speed is an asset here.

Ingredients

300g/10oz rosehips, stalks removed

300g/10oz golden caster sugar

Method

In a medium saucepan, bring 500ml/18fl oz water to the boil. Briefly mash the rosehips with a potato masher and immediately plunge into the boiling water. Bring the water back to the boil, take off the heat and leave the fruits to infuse for 15 minutes. Put both the rosehips and liquid into a jelly bag or strain through a muslin bag and allow the juice to drip through into a large, heatproof bowl for 30 minutes.

Using the same saucepan, bring another 500ml/18fl oz water to the boil, then add the rosehip pulp from the jelly bag, take off the heat, cover and allow to infuse for 10 minutes. Strain through the jelly bag or muslin cloth again into the bowl and allow all the liquid to drip through for an hour.

Wash out the saucepan and fill with the strained rosehip water. Place over a low heat and bring to a low simmer. Simmer for 20 minutes or until the liquid has reduced by one-third. Add the sugar, stirring until it dissolves, then pour into sterilised bottles. It will keep for up to 3 months in the fridge.

Glazed Rye and Rosehip Biscuits

Makes 16 | Vegan

Rye flour gives these delicately flavoured wholemeal biscuits a Scandinavian feel and a nutty texture, while the glazed rosehips provide a cherry-like tang.

Ingredients

185g/6¾oz wholemeal rye flour, plus extra for dusting

½ tsp baking powder

25g/1oz unrefined icing sugar, sifted

5 tbsp vegetable oil

For the glaze

125ml/4¼fl oz Rosehip Syrup (p.211)

2 dessertspoons cornflour

16–20 frozen rosehips (see Tip)

Method

Combine the flour, baking powder and icing sugar in a bowl and stir well. Gradually add in the oil and 2 tablespoons of water, then combine with a wooden spoon or your fingers to form a ball of dough. Don't overwork the dough by handling it too much. Wrap the dough in greaseproof paper or waxed paper and place in the fridge for 30 minutes.

Preheat the oven to 180°C/160°C fan/350°F and line a large baking tray with baking parchment.

Carefully roll out the dough on a clean, lightly floured surface to about 5mm/¼in thick. If it breaks or falls apart, just press it back together.

Cut the dough into rectangles or diamond shapes about 4cm/1½in wide and 7cm/2¾in long (this is just a guideline size, don't worry about getting it exact). Use a fish slice or slim knife to lift the biscuits and place them on the baking tray.

Bake for about 30 minutes or until golden. Remove from the oven, leave for 10 minutes, then transfer to a cooling rack to cool completely. At this stage you can store the biscuits in an airtight container for a week until ready to glaze.

For the glaze, blend 1 tablespoon of the rosehip syrup and the cornflour in a small bowl until smooth. In a small saucepan, heat the remaining syrup and, when hot but not boiling, pour into the bowl with the cornflour, mix, then pour back into the saucepan. Simmer over a low heat, stirring or whisking constantly, for a few minutes, until the mixture is nice and thick. You can store this in a sterilised jar in the fridge and use within 1 month.

When ready to assemble the biscuits, remove the rosehips from the freezer and, with a sharp knife, remove the ends and cut in half, lengthways. Carefully scoop out the seeds (the handle end of a narrow teaspoon is useful for this) and gently scrape inside the surface of the flesh to remove any remaining hairs.

Spread a little rosehip glaze across the top of each biscuit and stick a couple of rosehip halves cut side down onto the glaze. Spoon some extra glaze over each fruit and leave to dry. Store in an airtight container and best eaten within 2–3 days.

Tip

Using frozen rosehips helps preserve the vitamin C, as well as keeping the shape of the hips as you scoop out the centre.

Rosehip Fondant Biscuits

Makes 12

These delicious biscuits are buttery, crumbly and surprisingly filling for their size. They're sandwiched together with a creamy, fruity rosehip fondant and you'll need to use large hips like Japanese rosehips (*Rosa rugosa*, pictured on p.105) to get the best results.

Ingredients

125g/4½oz very soft butter

50g/2oz soft brown sugar

125g/4½oz plain flour

25g/1oz cornflour

For the fondant filling

50g/2oz white chocolate, finely chopped

30g/1oz frozen or semi-defrosted Japanese rosehip flesh from 90g/3oz whole Japanese rosehips (see Tip)

50g/2oz thick double cream

1 dessertspoon unrefined icing sugar

Method

Start by preparing the filling. Place the chopped chocolate in a heatproof bowl and put aside.

Place the rosehip flesh, cream and icing sugar in a blender and blend until smooth. If you don't have a blender, finely chop the flesh then add it to the cream and icing sugar and stir together. Place the cream mixture in a small saucepan over a low heat and heat until it starts to simmer at the edges. Do not boil; the mixture just needs to be hot enough to melt the chocolate. Pour the hot mixture over the chocolate and leave for 1 minute. Stir well, then leave to cool in the fridge until firm – about 1 hour.

Preheat the oven to 190°C/170°C fan/375°F. Grease a baking tray with a little butter or line it with baking parchment.

Put the butter, soft brown sugar, plain flour and cornflour in a bowl and beat together, or place in a food processor and blend until smooth. Take about half a dessertspoon of mixture at a time and roll between your fingers into a flat patty, about 3½cm/1¾in wide and 1cm/½in thick. Alternatively, divide the mixture in half, then half again and make 6 biscuits out of each batch. This mixture doesn't mind being handled a lot.

Spread the biscuits across the baking tray. Bake in the centre of the oven for 15 minutes or until lightly golden and firm. Cool on the baking tray for 5 minutes then transfer to a cooling rack.

Once the biscuits are cool, sandwich together with a generous amount of fondant filling. Store for up to 1 week in an airtight container in the fridge if you want the fondant firm, otherwise you can keep them at room temperature.

Tip

I find it easiest to scrape the flesh off when the fruits are frozen or semi-defrosted, so the ball of seeds doesn't fall apart and can be discarded, and the flesh doesn't go too mushy. This also helps preserve the nutrients. If you end up with more than 30g/1oz of rosehip flesh, the extra can be stirred into the biscuit mix.

Dark Rosehip Chocolates

Makes 10 | Vegan and gluten-free

I love discovering the red flecks of rosehip flesh as I bite into one of these: they're a simple and disarming match of tangy fruit nestled in firm dark chocolate. If you still have rosehips in the freezer at Valentine's Day, these make a great present for loved ones. This recipe is best created using large rosehips, like those from Japanese roses (*Rosa rugosa*, pictured on p.105), as there is more flesh on them to use.

Ingredients

40g/1½oz Japanese rosehip flesh (from around 110g/4oz whole Japanese rosehips – see Tip on p.215)

125g/4½oz vegan dark chocolate (minimum 70% cocoa solids), broken into pieces

Method

Chop the rosehip flesh a little, to ensure that you don't have any overlarge pieces of flesh or fruit skin.

To melt the chocolate, place it in a heatproof bowl over a saucepan of simmering water. Make sure the bowl doesn't touch the water. Once the chocolate has almost melted, stir in the rosehip flesh.

Pour into chocolate moulds or line a dish with greaseproof paper and spoon in the mixture. Leave to cool, then cut into chunks or peel out of the moulds. Store in an airtight container in a cool place, or in the fridge, and eat within 5 days.

Rowan Berries

Sorbus aucuparia (Rosaceae)

Adorned with clusters of orangey-red berries, the rowan tree stands tall, demanding attention. Rowan is often rebuffed because of its bitter tang, yet I love its exquisite, complex flavour – perfect for bittersweet, warming desserts. The berries do need to be cooked though to be fully appreciated (and digested).

In the UK, rowans exist happily in towns, cities and green spaces but most naturally thrive on mountain sides. Across Europe, Asia and North America, you'll find them in high-altitude places and they've been introduced in New Zealand and Argentina, too. In early autumn, their orange, just-ripe berries are perfect for marmalade (p.224). As winter draws in, the glorious leaves begin to curl and the berries shrivel and deepen to red; this is when they have the most flavour. When gathering these rich fruits, I always make sure to leave plenty for the birds who devour them as temperatures plummet and frosts descend. Crammed full of vitamin C, sorbic acid (once cooked), fibre and antioxidants, their benefits go far beyond deliciousness.

Main identifying features

Rowan trees grow up to 20m/65ft tall (though they can also prosper as shrubs) with long, narrow leaves growing opposite or alternate to one another, with one at the tip. The small, orangey-red berries grow in clusters, each berry just ½–1cm/¼in across.

When to forage

Early autumn to early winter.

Where to forage

Gardens, parks, hillsides and mountains.

How to forage

In autumn, pick clusters of berries by hand or with scissors while firm, then soften them in the freezer. After the first frost, pick the berries when soft, darker and (sometimes) shrivelled.

Cautions

Raw rowan berries can cause indigestion or lead to kidney damage due to the presence of parasorbic acid. Freezing (or picking after the first frost), then cooking them makes them safe to eat, digestible and more palatable.

If you pick rowan berries before the first frost, you can freeze then thaw them to make them a little sweeter.

Little Pinky Rowan Biscuits

Makes 20–24

These simple biscuits have a complex flavour twist thanks to a tiny bit of Rowan Berry Marmalade (p.224) placed in the centre of each one. A real treat to bite into, the name refers to using your little (pinky) finger to make the dip in the middle.

Ingredients

125g/4½oz butter, softened

65g/2½oz golden caster sugar

125g/4½oz plain flour

25g/1oz cornflour

½ tsp pure vanilla extract

30g/1oz (1 heaped tbsp) Rowan Berry Marmalade (p.224)

Method

Preheat the oven to 190°C/170°C fan/375°F and line two large baking trays with baking parchment.

Put the butter, sugar, flour, cornflour and vanilla extract in a large bowl and beat together, or place in a food processor and blend until smooth. Take about a dessertspoon of mixture and roll between your fingers into a flat patty, about 3½cm/1¾in wide and 1cm/½in thick. Repeat with all the mixture – you should be able to make 20–24 biscuits.

Place on the baking trays, spacing them well apart as they will spread. Lightly push your little finger into the centre of each biscuit, to about two-thirds of the depth of the biscuit to make a dip. Using the narrow end of a teaspoon, put a little dab of rowan marmalade into each hole. Place the trays in the fridge for 10 minutes, then bake in the centre of the oven for 15–20 minutes or until lightly golden and firm. Cool on the baking tray for 5 minutes then transfer to a cooling rack. Store in an airtight container and eat within 1 week.

Rowan Berry Marmalade

Makes approx. 350–400g/12–14oz
Vegan and gluten-free

A pot of this is irresistibly good and uncannily like rustic, orange marmalade, though a little richer thanks to the dark sugar and the curious tangy flavour of rowan berries.

Ingredients

250g/9oz rowan berries

250g/9oz sweet apples, cored and chopped

250g/9oz soft brown sugar

Method

Discard all the stalks (this will take time but is worth it) and place the berries and apples in a medium saucepan. Add 150ml/5fl oz water (it may not cover the fruits completely) and bring to the boil. Cover and simmer for 30 minutes, or until the rowan berries are soft. Drain the fruit and liquid through a sieve into a large bowl. Next, mash the fruits with a wooden spoon through the sieve into the same bowl, so as much as the fruit pulp as possible is gained from the fruits. Put the liquid and pulp aside and discard any seeds and fibre left in the sieve.

Wash and dry the saucepan, add the sugar and warm over a medium heat for 5 minutes, stirring occasionally. When the sugar is browning and starting to caramelise, take off the heat and immediately add the fruit pulp and liquid and stir in – be careful as it may spit while bubbling. Place back on the heat and bring to a simmer for 5–10 minutes, until the mixture has reduced a little, stirring occasionally to make sure the fruit pulp doesn't burn.

Test to see if it is set (see Tip on p.172) then, when ready, pour into sterilised jars while still hot, and seal. Keeps for 6 months in the fridge.

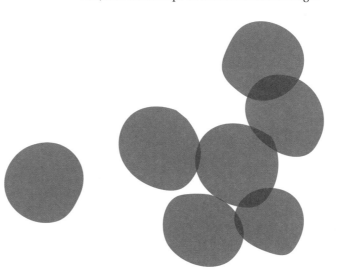

Rowan Berries in Syrup

Makes 350g/12oz | Vegan and gluten-free

These are lovely straight from the jar, though even better served with the Chocolate Panna Cotta on p.227. They mature with time and are best after a week; they can be kept in the fridge for several months.

Ingredients

120g/4¼oz golden granulated sugar

150g/5oz rowan berries, stalks removed

Method

Place 150ml/5fl oz water and the sugar in a medium saucepan and slowly bring to the boil over a low heat, stirring to dissolve the sugar. Lower the heat, add the rowan berries and simmer for 10 minutes. Pour into a sterilised jar and seal. They will keep for up to 3 months in the fridge.

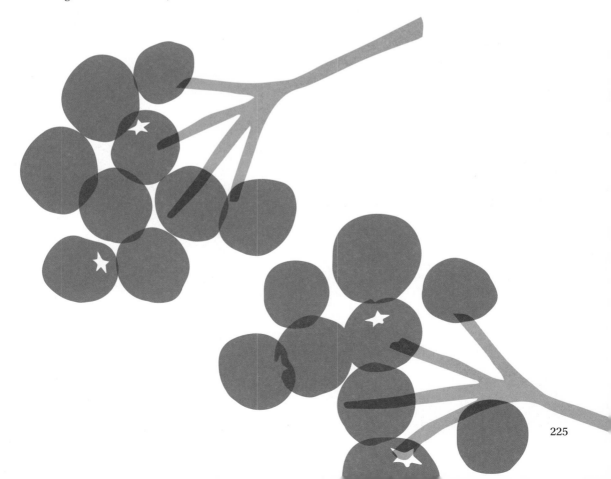

Chocolate Panna Cotta with Rowan Berries

Serves 4 | Gluten-free

This softly textured, creamy chocolate panna cotta is the perfect companion to the unique flavour and tart bite of rowan berries. I love using carrageen seaweed for desserts (and also in my Elderflower and Carrageen Refreshers, p.92). Its mild flavour, health benefits and natural setting ability are winners for me – though you can use gelatine instead, if you prefer.

Ingredients

8g/¼oz dried carrageen seaweed (or 25g/1oz fresh carrageen seaweed; see Tip on p.92)

250ml/8½fl oz full-fat milk

400ml/13½fl oz double cream

50g/2oz golden caster sugar

1 tbsp cocoa powder

4 tbsp Rowan Berries in Syrup (p.225)

Method

Place the carrageen in a small saucepan, pour in the milk and leave to soak for 10 minutes. Slowly bring to a low simmer over a low heat and simmer for 8 minutes, then strain through a jelly bag or muslin cloth. Allow all the liquid to drip through; give the bag a squeeze if it needs some help, which I find it always does.

Return the thickened liquid to the pan, along with the cream, sugar and cocoa powder and stir well. Bring to an almost simmer – watching it carefully until it just starts to quiver. Pour into 4 ramekins and leave to set for a few hours at room temperature or overnight in the fridge.

When ready to serve, place the ramekins in a dish of boiling water and carefully slice around the edge of each one before turning onto individual plates. Decorate each panna cotta with a tablespoon of rowan berries in syrup.

Rowan Marmalade Pudding

Serves 6–8

This is wild comfort food at its best: a warming dessert with a toffee-coloured sponge, a thick, sweet sauce and the sharp autumn flavour of rowan berries. As the days get colder and the nights draw in, it's the perfect way to finish off an evening meal.

Ingredients

100g/3½oz plain flour, sifted

75g/2¾oz wholemeal flour, sifted

1½ tsp baking powder, sifted

60g/2¼oz dark brown muscovado sugar

110ml/3¾fl oz full-fat milk

50g/2oz Rowan Berry Marmalade (p.224)

1 large free-range egg

1 tsp vanilla extract (optional)

50g/2oz butter, melted, plus 1 tbsp, softened

175g/6oz chopped dates

single cream, to serve (optional)

For the sauce

300ml/10fl oz boiling water

250g/9oz Rowan Berry Marmalade (p.224)

Method

Preheat the oven to 190°C/170°C fan/375°F and grease a 1½-litre/2¾-pint ovenproof dish.

Add the flours, baking powder and muscovado sugar to a large bowl.

To a medium bowl or measuring jug, add the milk, 50g/2oz rowan marmalade, egg, vanilla extract, if using, and melted butter and whisk together until smooth. Pour into the sugar and flour mix, combine well then fold in the chopped dates. Spoon into the dish and distribute the tablespoon of softened butter across the top in little dots.

For the sauce, whisk together the boiling water and rowan marmalade. Pour the sauce over the pudding and bake for 45 minutes, or until the top of the pudding is springy and spongy. Serve warm, on its own or with cream.

Haw Berries

Crataegus monogyna (Rosaceae)

The gnarled shape of a hawthorn tree will tell you which way the wind has predominantly blown over the decades. In spring and summer, these trees' twisting branches are hidden by abundant leaves and flowers, but as their foliage falls and berries brighten, their true form is revealed. Numerous varieties grow across the world, but this species (common hawthorn, *Crataegus monogyna*) is native to Europe, North Africa and some parts of the Middle East. It has also been introduced across North America, Australasia, Argentina and the Cape Provinces.

Shaped like miniscule apples, the berries even taste a little like apple peel when bitten into. Raw, they are edible but unimpressive; cooking and sweetening the berries reduces them to a rich pulp with a deep, tangy flavour that I adore. They've also long been used to improve heart health as they can help to lower blood pressure and smooth out irregular heartbeats, and are full of vitamins – including A, B1, B2, B3, B17 and C. These berries pack a lot of goodness into a tiny package.

Main identifying features

Hawthorn trees can grow over 4m/13ft tall, with thorny, often gnarled branches. Clusters of small orangey-red berries turn red when ripe, and are often less than 1cm/½in across, each containing a surprisingly large, single stone. Leaves are crown-shaped with three lobes at the top and two lower lobes pointing outwards.

When to forage

Mid-autumn to early winter,

Where to forage

Deciduous woods, hedges or hilltops up to 600m/2,000ft.

How to forage

Pick the berries off with your fingers, or cut clusters and de-stalk at home. Berries are ready when dark red and soft to the touch.

Cautions

Haw berries can lower and modulate blood pressure, and should be eaten with caution and under the guidance of a medical herbalist if you are on heart medication, as they may interact with prescribed drugs.

Other notable varieties

Midland hawthorn (*Crataegus laevigata*)

Haw Berry and Star Anise Jam

Makes 350g/12oz | Vegan and gluten-free

This is a thick-textured jam, more like a mildly flavoured, dark red fruit purée. It's a great addition to my Haw Berry and Chocolate Baked Cheesecake (p.237), and I love how the star anise adds extra layers of sweetness and spice.

Ingredients

500g/1lb 2oz haw berries

4 star anise

approx. 240g/8¾oz soft brown sugar

Method

Place the haw berries, the star anise and 180ml/6¼fl oz water in a small saucepan. Bring to the boil, then cover and turn down to a low simmer for 15 minutes. Take off the heat.

Place a sieve over a large heatproof bowl – the sieve should fit snuggly within it. Pour the haws and liquid into the sieve. Remove and discard the star anise. Using the back of a wooden spoon, mash the fruits through the sieve. Do this for about 10 minutes to get as much fruit flesh as possible from the haws, leaving the seeds behind in the sieve.

Next, weigh the fruit pulp and add the sugar. There should be about 300g/10oz of pulp: for every 25g/1oz, add 20g/¾oz sugar. (So 300g/10oz fruit pulp will require 240g/8½oz sugar.)

Place the fruit pulp and sugar in a medium saucepan, bring to the boil and simmer for 5–10 minutes, until it reaches 105°C/221°F on a jam thermometer. (If you don't have a thermometer, you can use the 'setting test' to check the jam has reached the right consistency: see Tip on p.172.)

Pour into a sterilised jar while still hot, then seal. It will keep for up to 6 months in the fridge.

Haw Delight

Makes approx. 45 | Vegan and gluten-free

These tempting squares of haw delight carry a delicate flavour of haw berries in a softly textured jelly. I just adore the way they melt in the mouth. This recipe requires watching the pot for an hour or so, so is a good one for a rainy autumnal day.

Ingredients

500g/1lb 2oz haw berries

2 tbsp lemon juice

800g/1lb 12oz golden granulated or caster sugar

120g/4¼oz cornflour

1 heaped tsp cream of tartar

For the coating

30g/1oz cornflour, sifted, plus extra to store

50g/2oz unrefined icing sugar, sifted, plus extra to store

Method

In a medium saucepan, place the haw berries, 1 tablespoon of the lemon juice and 450ml/¾ pint water. Bring to the boil, then simmer, covered, over a low heat for 30 minutes.

Allow to cool slightly, before mashing the fruits a little with a potato masher and placing in a jelly bag over a medium-sized bowl. Leave to drip through for a couple of hours, then measure the juice and add enough water to make it up to 375ml/13fl oz if needed.

Lightly oil a 20cm/8in square tin.

To make the haw delight, you'll be heating two large, heavy-bottomed saucepans (one about 20cm/8in wide x 10cm/4in deep, and a larger one about 23cm/9in wide x 10cm/4in deep) simultaneously. To the smaller saucepan, add the sugar, the remaining 1 tablespoon of lemon juice and the haw juice and stir over a medium heat until the sugar has dissolved. Bring to the boil and heat to 118°C/244°F on a sugar thermometer, without stirring. This will take about 15 minutes. When it reaches temperature, take off the heat and put aside.

Meanwhile, to the second, larger saucepan, add the 120g/4¼oz cornflour and the cream of tartar, then gradually add 450ml/¾ pint water, stirring, until the mixture changes from stiff to liquid and is well combined. Warm over a low heat, continually whisking, until the mixture resembles a thick, white paste.

At this point, gradually pour the sugar mixture into the larger pan and whisk until combined. Bring to the boil, then lower the heat and gently simmer for 1–1½ hours, stirring regularly to check the sugar hasn't stuck to the bottom of the pan. Once the mixture becomes stringy if pulled between two spoons, pour it into the prepared tin, spread to an even layer and leave to set for a few hours, or overnight, at room temperature.

Once set, make the coating by combining the cornflour and icing sugar, then sprinkle it onto a large chopping board or large piece of baking parchment. Tip the block of haw delight onto it, then cut it into 7 strips. Toss each strip in the coating, then cut them all into squares and toss again until all the sides are coated; this will help them keep longer and make them easier to handle. Store in layers in a breathable box at room temperature, with extra icing sugar blend between each layer, for up to 1 month. After a while, the haw delight will become slightly sticky, so dust with more of the icing sugar blend before serving.

Haw Berry and Chocolate Baked Cheesecake

Serves 8–10 | Can be made gluten-free

This unusual and earthy cheesecake is rather scrumptious. It's enriched with fruity Haw Berry and Star Anise Jam (p.233), which combines beautifully with its soft chocolate base.

For the base

65g/2½oz butter, softened

45g/1¾oz light brown sugar

2 large free-range eggs, beaten

55g/2oz plain flour (or gluten-free flour)

50g/2oz porridge oats (gluten-free if necessary)

1 tbsp cocoa powder

For the topping

175g/6oz Haw Berry and Star Anise Jam (p.233)

1 tsp cornflour

300g/10oz full-fat soft cheese

75g/2¾oz golden caster sugar

75g/2¾oz natural yoghurt

Method

Preheat the oven to 180°C/160°C fan/350°F and grease a 20cm/8in loose-bottomed cake tin.

Start by making the base. In a bowl, cream together the butter and sugar until light and fluffy. Add a quarter of the beaten egg (put the rest aside for the topping) and beat to combine, then stir in the flour, oats and cocoa powder. Thoroughly mix together, before pressing into the tin. The base will be quite thin, so take your time to press into the edges either with the back of a spoon or clean fingers.

Now, make the topping. Place 100g/3½oz of the haw berry jam in a small saucepan with the cornflour. Stir over a medium heat until bubbling, then lower the heat and let the jam thicken for a couple of minutes, stirring occasionally. Put aside and leave to cool.

In a bowl, whisk the soft cheese and golden caster sugar together. Next beat in the yoghurt, then beat in the remaining egg left over from the base, a little at a time.

Gently spread the remaining 75g/2½oz of haw berry jam across the chocolate base, then spoon over half the cheese mixture. Use a teaspoon to drop spots of the thickened, cooled haw berry jam across the cheese mixture (using about half of the jam). Pour in the remaining cheese mixture, spread evenly and make dots with the remaining jam, dragging the teaspoon a little to make swirled shapes. Bake for 40–45 minutes or until the cheesecake is set but still with a wobble in the centre. Turn off the oven, leaving the cake inside for a further 1 hour, then take out and allow to cool to room temperature before serving. Keeps well in the fridge for up to 4 days.

Haw Fruit Leather

Makes 1 large sheet
Gluten-free and dairy-free

This is my go-to fruit leather when I'm struggling to get through a slow morning or sluggish afternoon. I just cut off a small square or a sliver and imagine the tangy sweetness reactivating my brain as I chew.

Ingredients

450g/1lb haw berries, stalks removed

450g/1lb sweet apples, roughly chopped (core and all)

3 tbsp honey

Method

Place the fruits and 350ml/11¾fl oz water in a medium saucepan and bring to the boil. Cover and simmer for 15 minutes, or until the fruits are soft. Strain the liquid through a sieve or fine colander into a large bowl. Allow the fruit pulp in the sieve to cool then, using a wooden spoon, mash the fruit pulp through the sieve into the bowl. Continue until you have as much pulp as possible, then stir in the honey.

Once you've extracted all the pulp, you can dry the fruit leather in two ways. If you have a dehydrator, dry as per machine instructions, then cut into pieces or strips and store in a sterilised jar (or wrapped in baking parchment) at room temperature.

Alternatively, preheat the oven to 140°C/ 120°C fan/275°F and line a 20x40cm/8x16in baking tray with baking parchment, including part way up the sides.

Pour the fruit pulp into the tray, spread evenly and bake for 4–5 hours, until the fruit is slightly tacky to the touch, without staying stuck to your fingers, and peels away easily from the parchment. If the fruit is drying unevenly, turn the tray around in the oven, or be prepared to slice off any crisped edges when done. Peel the leather off the parchment, leave to cool, then cut into pieces or strips and store as above.

Keeps for up to 1 year.

Winter

As the temperature drops,
life slows down: trees are
bare and plants wither in
the quiet of winter. Yet, deep
in the ground, roots subtly
sweeten and mature. Their
warming sustenance makes
for substantial meals and
proper puddings, full
of the goodness of the soil.
The descent into winter
is the perfect time to harvest
this bounty, before light
and warmth returns.

Burdock Roots

Arctium lappa (Asteraceae)

The large, downy leaves of burdock grow in surprising places, aided by the plant's sticky, hooked 'burs'. These burs attach fast and travel far on animals or clothing – a clever way for burdock to scatter its seeds. Its long root is prized as a vegetable across the world, though I love bringing out its mild, nutty flavour in drinks and desserts.

Native across Europe and Asia, introduced to North America and parts of Australasia and cultivated in Asia, burdock is a biennial plant – its life span being just 2 years. Amiable farmers have been happy for me to dig up these weeds from their land in the past (make sure you always ask – and bring a sturdy fork or spade, as these long roots prefer stony ground). It's renowned for its skin-soothing qualities for ailments including eczema, acne, rashes, dermatitis and psoriasis, as it helps support the liver and kidneys and can also help purify the blood and lower blood sugar. Burdock roots provide potassium, calcium, phosphorous and protein: there's a lot of goodness growing underground.

Main identifying features

Burdock plants grow up to 2m/6½ft tall. Its stems can be green or purple-tinged with a furry, downy feel, while leaves are large, heart-shaped and furry and their undersides are always paler (almost white). Its purple flowers look like thistles, but are soft to the touch, and seedheads are spherical and covered in tiny, catching hooks. Roots grow up to 1m/3ft long.

When to forage

Early autumn to late winter (though it's harder to dig in the cold, hard earth of mid to late winter).

Where to forage

Wastelands, waysides, near buildings, scrublands, gardens, fields and the edges of woodland – burdock favours heavy, rocky soil.

How to forage

Use a large fork or spade and dig around the base of the leaves to loosen the plant, then dig as deep as you can to attempt to lift out as much of the root as possible.

Cautions

Use with caution and with the guidance of a medical herbalist if you're diabetic or have blood sugar issues. Some people have a skin reaction to the leaves. In the UK, permission is needed from the landowner to dig up roots: check the laws in your country before uprooting.

Other notable varieties

Lesser burdock (*Arctium minus*)
Woolly burdock (*Arctium tomentosum*)

Burdock roots grow deep into the ground: you'll need a fork or spade (and the landowner's permission) to dig for them.

Burdock Beer

Makes 2–2½ litres/3½–4½ pints
Vegan and gluten-free

Dark and rich with a frothy top, this slightly alcoholic fizzy drink is a fantastic celebration of the humble burdock root. Ready in just over a week, drink it as it is or use it in Burdock Beer and Chocolate Cake (p.248) or Burdock Beer Sponge (see opposite).

Ingredients

40g/1½oz burdock roots, scrubbed and roughly chopped

225g/8oz dark brown sugar

2 tbsp molasses (optional, add for a darker and richer beer)

juice of ½ lemon

5g/⅛oz dried yeast

Method

In a large saucepan, add the burdock roots and 2¼ litres/4 pints water, cover and simmer for 30 minutes. Remove from the heat and strain through a sieve into a large bowl, discarding the burdock roots. Add the sugar and molasses, if using, to the hot liquid and stir to dissolve, then add the lemon juice. Set aside to cool.

In a jug, dissolve the yeast in a little warm water and leave to become frothy. When the burdock root liquid is room temperature, pour it into a large bowl or clean bucket and add the yeast.

Cover with a large plate, clean cloth or lid, allowing a little air to escape, and leave for a week before bottling. It may need a further few days to get to a good flavour and fizziness, though do check regularly and refrigerate to stop the fermenting if the bubbling looks like it may get out of hand! Store in sterilised bottles for up to 1 year.

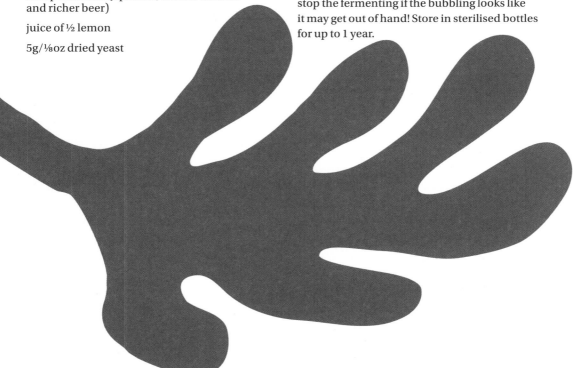

Burdock Beer Sponge

Serves 8–10

This sponge is great as a simple, malty cake in its own right, though I originally created it as a base for my Dandelion and Burdock Tiramisu (p.262). It freezes well, too, so you can pull it out when a sweet craving catches you off guard.

Ingredients

110g/4oz butter, softened

200g/7oz dark muscovado sugar

2 large free-range eggs

175g/6oz self-raising flour (or 175g/6oz plain flour plus 2½ tsp baking powder)

¼ tsp baking powder

1 tsp bicarbonate of soda

200ml/6¾fl oz Burdock Beer (see opposite page)

Method

Preheat the oven to 180°C/160°C fan/350°F and line two 20cm/8in cake tins with baking parchment.

Add the butter, sugar and eggs to a large bowl. From a good height (to add some air), sift in the flour, baking powder and bicarbonate of soda. Whisk to combine with an electric whisk to create a creamy mixture.

Gradually stir in the beer until the mixture is smooth, then pour into the cake tins. Bake in the middle of the oven for 30 minutes, then leave to cool in the tin for 10 minutes before turning out onto a cooling rack. Store in an airtight container for up to 5 days.

Tip

If intending to make Dandelion and Burdock Tiramisu (p.262), you'll need just one of these cakes and it's best to dry it out a little before using. Cut the cake into about 12 pieces and place back in the tin randomly so there is breathing space between the pieces. Place in the still warm, but turned off, oven and leave for 1–2 hours or overnight to dry out further. This stage isn't essential but will help when you are dipping the sponge into the Dandelion Coffee Syrup (p.255) for the tiramisu.

Burdock Beer and Chocolate Cake with Muscovado Yoghurt

Serves 8–10

This is a beautifully moist, rich chocolate cake with background tones of Burdock Beer (p.246). I love to cut a large slice of it and enjoy just as it is, but it's also divine dressed up with the slight sourness of this creamy yoghurt sauce that isn't overly sweet or rich.

Ingredients

110g/4oz butter, softened

220g/7¾ oz dark muscovado sugar

2 large free-range eggs

25g/1oz cocoa powder

175g/6oz self-raising flour (or 175g/6oz plain flour plus 2½ tsp baking powder)

¼ tsp baking powder

1 tsp bicarbonate of soda

200ml/6¾fl oz Burdock Beer (p.246)

For the yoghurt sauce (optional)

300g/10oz full-fat creamy natural yoghurt

2 tbsp Burdock Beer (p.246)

90g/3¼oz dark muscovado sugar

Method

Preheat the oven to 180°C/160°C fan/350°F and line a 20cm/8in cake tin with baking parchment.

Add the butter, sugar, eggs and cocoa powder to a large bowl. From a good height (to add some air), sift in the flour, baking powder and bicarbonate of soda. Whisk to combine with an electric whisk to create a creamy mixture.

Gradually stir in the beer until the mixture is smooth, then pour into the cake tin. Bake for 40 minutes, or until the cake is firm and springs back when touched. Turn out onto a cooling rack and leave to cool. Store in an airtight container at room temperature for up to 5 days.

For the sauce, in a medium bowl or jug, mix the ingredients together and refrigerate till needed. Take out of the fridge 30 minutes before serving to allow the flavours to fully come through. The sauce keeps well for up to 3 days in the fridge, but is easy to make on demand.

Honeycombed Burdock Roots

Makes 65g/2½oz
Gluten-free and dairy-free

Reminiscent of honeycomb, this recipe turns burdock roots into sweet, crunchy and chewy, honeyed treats with a hint of rooty goodness. Enjoy them as a snack on their own or crush them to scatter over Dandelion and Burdock Tiramisu (p.262).

Ingredients

150g/5⅛oz burdock roots, scrubbed, peeled and chopped into 5mm–1cm/¼–½in pieces

2 tbsp local runny honey

45g/1¾oz soft brown sugar

Method

Place the burdock roots in a steamer basket over a saucepan of simmering water and steam for 5 minutes, then put aside to cool and dry out.

Preheat the oven to 170°C/150°C fan/325°F and line a baking tray with baking parchment.

In a small saucepan, add the honey and burdock roots and heat over a high heat. Stir with a wooden spoon and, once bubbling, cook for 5 minutes before adding the sugar. Stir to coat the roots thoroughly, then take off the heat and tip the roots onto the baking tray, spreading them out into an even layer.

Bake for 50 minutes to 1 hour (checking every 15 minutes and turning the pieces) or until the mixture is frothing up to at least double the height of the roots and all the moisture has evaporated. Turn off the oven and leave the roots inside to dry out further, for a few hours or overnight.

Break up and store in an airtight container at room temperature for up to 1 year. Eat as a snack or crush and use as an edible decoration. The roots may become sticky again with storage, in which case place them on a baking tray and warm in the oven for 10 minutes at 170°C/150°C fan/325°F. Then turn off the heat and let them cool completely before crushing them.

Dandelion Roots

Taraxacum officinale (Asteraceae)

Steady and continuous through all seasons, the toothed leaves of dandelions (best to pick in spring, see p.60) in winter show me where to plunge a trowel into the earth. While the leaves are no longer at their most tender, the roots are ready for digging up. Small and unassuming, when roasted these roots have a warming, coffee-like, almost chocolatey flavour that makes for some truly comforting winter sweets.

I often offer to 'weed' my friend Liz's allotment at this time of year, in order to gather these beauties. I sometimes find a pile of them on my doorstep, too – a gift from friends who have been weeding their gardens and know I'll appreciate these delicious roots. Growing widely across the world, dandelion roots can stimulate digestion, improve gut bacteria (through the presence of inulin), benefit the liver and help with skin conditions: all positive attributes for sluggish winters.

Main identifying features

Deeply toothed leaves grow from the base of the dandelion plant – look for these to know where to dig. Roots grow up to 20cm/8in long.

When to forage

Early autumn through to late winter.

Where to forage

Dandelions are extremely easily found in sunny areas, gardens, growing up between pavements, in parks, grassy fields and road verges.

How to forage

Dig around the base of the leaves and use your fingers, a knife or trowel to scrape towards the bottom of the root. It is not easy to pull the roots out intact; often they will snap halfway down, but with a little patience and deeper digging, you can remove a whole root.

How to roast

280g/9¾oz fresh roots will make around 50g/2oz roasted. First, clean the roots and pat them dry, then lay them out on in a warm, dry place for 2–3 days. Finely chop the roots, then bake in a preheated oven at 180°C/160°C fan/350°F for 30–40 minutes, until dark brown, turning once or twice during cooking to make sure they roast evenly. Once cool, store in an airtight, sterilised jar at room temperature for up to 6 months.

Cautions

In the UK, permission is needed from the landowner to dig up roots: check the laws in your country before uprooting.

Dandelion Coffee

Makes 400ml/13½fl oz | Vegan and gluten-free

This simple, caffeine-free drink has a roasted chocolate fragrance and a mildly bitter aftertaste. It's lovely drunk alongside a morning snack of Candied Dandelion Root Citrus Peel (p.260).

Ingredients

2 tbsp roasted dandelion roots (see roasting instructions on p.252)

Method

Grind the roasted dandelion roots in a coffee or spice grinder, then place in a small saucepan with 500ml/18fl oz water. Bring to a simmer over a low heat and allow to gently bubble for 10 minutes. Strain through a tea strainer, muslin cloth or fine sieve, discard the roots, then pour the coffee into mugs, adding milk and sweetener, if you like.

Dandelion Coffee Syrup

Makes 200ml/6¾fl oz | Vegan and gluten-free

This delectable syrup is used to soak the Burdock Beer Sponge (p.247) in my Dandelion and Burdock Tiramisu recipe (p.262). It also makes a great addition to bitter cocktails (or mocktails!).

Ingredients

1 tbsp roasted dandelion roots (see roasting instructions on p.252)

150g/5oz soft brown sugar

Method

Grind the roasted dandelion roots in a coffee or spice grinder and place in a small saucepan with 175ml/6fl oz water. Bring to the boil and gently simmer for 10 minutes, then strain through a tea strainer or muslin cloth, discarding the roots. There should be about 100–125ml/3½–4¼fl oz liquid.

Pour back into the (cleaned) pan and add the sugar. Stir over a low heat until the sugar has dissolved, then bring to a simmer and immediately take off the heat. Allow to cool fully, then store in a sterilised jar or bottle for up to 3 months in the fridge.

Roasted Dandelion and Almond Thins

Makes 25–30 | Vegan

Chewy and crispy, these thins offset the deep flavour of roasted dandelion with either a sweet citrussy or dark dandelion icing. A great chocolate-free alternative to finish off a meal.

Ingredients

75g/2¾oz plain wheat or rye flour, sifted

25g/1oz wholemeal flour, sifted

¼ tsp bicarbonate of soda, sifted

3½ tbsp ground roasted dandelion roots (see roasting instructions on p.252)

55g/2oz ground almonds

125g/4½oz soft brown sugar

100ml/3½fl oz rapeseed oil

For the icing

60g/2¼oz unrefined icing sugar

1 tbsp lemon juice

1–2 tsp finely ground roasted dandelion roots (see roasting instructions on p.252; optional)

Method

Add the flours and bicarbonate of soda into a large bowl, then stir in the 3½ tablespoons of ground dandelion roots, the ground almonds, soft brown sugar, oil and 2 tablespoons of water and combine well. The mixture will be quite wet, though firm enough to pat into a loose dough.

Place on a piece of baking parchment and, using the sides of the paper, shape into an oblong about 20cm/8in long and 10cm/4in wide. Wrap the dough tightly in the paper and place in the freezer. You can now leave it for at least 2 hours or up to 3 months in the freezer, until you want to make the thins (seal the wrapped dough in a bag or container if you're keeping it in the freezer for more than a few hours).

Preheat the oven to 180°C/160°C fan/350°F and grease a couple of baking trays.

Take the dough out of the freezer, unwrap and finely slice across the width to make about 25–30 thins, each 10cm/4in wide. Transfer to the baking trays and bake for 10 minutes, then take out and leave to cool on the trays for another 10 minutes, before moving them onto a cooling rack to cool completely.

I like to dip the tips of these into icing, once they've firmed up. In a small shallow bowl, combine the icing sugar and lemon juice until smooth. If you wish, decant half the mixture into another bowl and mix the ground dandelion roots into it. You now have two contrasting icings to dip the tips in, or to drizzle over the thins. Once dipped, lay the thins back on the cooling rack to drip dry and, once the icing has set, store in an airtight container at room temperature. These are best eaten within 5–7 days.

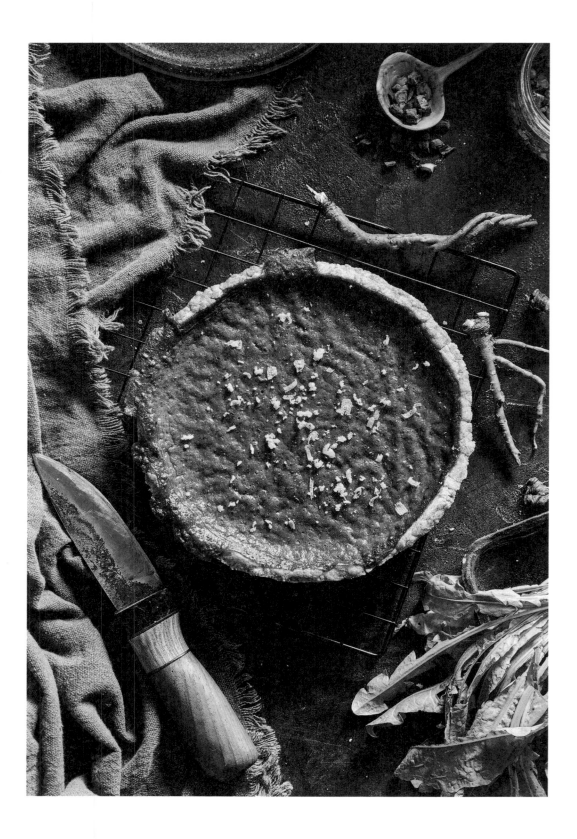

Roasted Dandelion and Orange Pie

Serves 10–12 | Vegan

A gorgeously smooth and light vegan pie with a crumbly crust, this dessert has a flavour reminiscent of chocolate. The bittersweetness of the dandelion root is perfectly balanced with a lingering orangey-ness throughout. It was inspired by my mum's orange pastry mince pies that she makes for Christmas.

For the pastry

100g/3½oz wholemeal flour, sifted

100g/3½oz plain flour, sifted

40g/1½oz unrefined icing sugar, sifted

6 tbsp vegetable or olive oil (or half of each)

2 tbsp fresh orange juice (from ½–1 orange)

zest of 1 unwaxed orange

For the filling

25g/1oz cornflour

90g/3¼oz soft brown sugar

450ml/¾ pint soya milk or plant-based milk

35ml/1fl oz fresh orange juice (from 1–2 oranges)

1 dessertspoon olive oil

3 tbsp finely ground roasted dandelion roots (see roasting instructions on p.252)

Method

Preheat the oven to 180°C/160°C fan/350°F and grease a 20cm/8in, loose-bottomed cake tin.

To make the pastry, add the flours and icing sugar to a large bowl, mix well and add the oil, orange juice and zest and mix to form a dough. Roll into a ball, cover with greaseproof paper or waxed paper and place in the fridge for 30 minutes or more.

To make the filling, mix the cornflour and soft brown sugar in a medium bowl and add enough milk to make a smooth paste. In a small saucepan, add the remaining milk, orange juice, oil and ground dandelion roots, followed by the cornflour mix and mix well. Stir continuously over a medium–high heat until bubbling, then turn down the heat a little and continue to stir for 5 minutes while the mixture thickens. Set aside.

Place the ball of dough in the cake tin and use your fingers to spread the dough evenly across the base and up the sides. Line with a sheet of baking parchment and fill with baking beans or uncooked rice, then bake for 10 minutes. Remove the paper and beans or rice before pouring in the filling and baking for a further 20–30 minutes, or until the pastry is browned and the filling is almost set; it will set further when cooled. Allow to cool completely before cutting and serving. Keep in the fridge in an airtight container for up to 4 days.

Candied Dandelion Root Citrus Peel

Makes 32 pieces | Vegan

My friend Liz described these little treats as having a curious flavour and being strangely addictive. They make perfect gifts, and I exchanged a bag of them for the chance to forage some dandelion roots from Liz's allotment. She ate them rather quickly, but they can keep for several months.

Ingredients

2 unwaxed oranges

175g/6oz golden caster sugar

75g/2¾oz soft brown sugar

2 tbsp ground roasted dandelion roots (see roasting instructions on p.252)

Method

First peel the oranges by cutting them in half, then quarters. Carefully peel off the skins and put the flesh aside for Roasted Dandelion and Orange Pie (p.259). Flatten the skin quarters and slice them each into 4 long strips.

Bring a medium saucepan of water (just enough water to cover the strips of peel) to the boil and add the peel, simmering for 5 minutes. Strain off the water and repeat with fresh water. Drain the water and put the twice-cooked peel onto a cooling rack to dry.

Meanwhile, place the sugars, 300ml/10fl oz water and ground dandelion roots into the saucepan. Cut a piece of baking parchment just big enough to act as a lid for the saucepan; this will help the peel cook evenly and allow the steam to escape. Bring the liquid to a simmer and place the peel into the saucepan, pressing them down a couple of times. Place the paper lid (also known as a cartouche) on top and leave to gently simmer for 1 hour.

Lift out the peel with a slotted spoon and place on a cooling rack with a tray underneath to catch the drips. Bring the remaining syrup left in the pan to the boil and simmer for 5 minutes or until reduced by about half, being careful not to let it burn. Remove from the heat and tip the peel back in the pan, stirring to coat, then use the slotted spoon to lift back out onto the cooling rack. Leave to dry out for up to 7 days on the cooling rack, then wrap in baking parchment and store in a dry place. The candied peel will keep for up to 4 months.

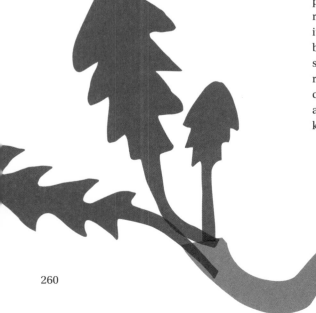

Dandelion and Burdock Tiramisu

Serves 8

This heavenly, multi-layered, pick-me-up dessert is made using various dandelion and burdock elements that can be prepared in advance, making it the perfect thing to assemble for a dinner party. Here in the UK, dandelion and burdock roots are a classic combination that have been used to create a fermented drink since the Middle Ages.

Ingredients

500g/1lb 2oz mascarpone cheese

1–2 tbsp brandy, to taste (optional; otherwise use 1 tbsp water)

2 tbsp dark brown sugar

100ml/3½fl oz Dandelion Coffee Syrup (p.255)

300g/10oz (1 cake) Burdock Beer Sponge (p.247)

For the topping

1 heaped tsp roasted dandelion roots (see roasting instructions on p.252)

20g/¾oz Honeycombed Burdock Roots (p.251)

Method

In a small bowl, combine the mascarpone, brandy (or water) and sugar and put aside.

Dilute the dandelion coffee syrup with 100ml/3½fl oz water and place in a shallow dish. Slice the burdock beer sponge into 12 pieces, then cut each slice into pieces lengthways to create skinny sponge fingers. Briefly dunk each piece of cake in the syrup and let drip for a few seconds before placing on the base of a 20cm/8in round or square dish. Continue until you have covered the base of the dish with a thin layer of cake.

Spoon over half of the mascarpone mixture, smoothing it out, then add a layer of the remaining cake (again dunking each piece in turn in the syrup), then the remaining mascarpone mixture. Leave to set in the fridge for at least a couple of hours so the flavours can mingle. Take out of the fridge 30 minutes before serving and add the topping.

For the topping, grind the roasted dandelion roots as finely as possible – in a pestle and mortar or a seed or coffee grinder – then sieve and collect the fine powder. (Use the larger pieces for another recipe in this section.) From a bit of a height, sprinkle the powdered dandelion roots over the top of the tiramisu. Next, crush the honeycombed burdock roots and sprinkle liberally over the top. Serve immediately.

Index

US Glossary

baking powder/bicarbonate of soda – baking soda

baking tray – baking sheet

biscuits – cookies

caster sugar – superfine sugar

desiccated coconut – shredded coconut

double cream – heavy cream

cornflour – corn starch

frying pan – skillet

icing – frosting

icing sugar – confectioners' sugar

jam – jelly

jelly – jello

plain flour – all-purpose flour

rapeseed oil – canola oil

rolled oats – oatmeal

self-raising flour – self-rising flour

treacle – molasses

Acknowledgements

This book is dedicated to my mum, for introducing me to the alchemy of baking and giving us too much sugar as children; and to my dad, for all our camping, walking and sailing adventures – I miss you. Together, you set the scene for *Wild and Sweet*.

And to my friend Martin for carelessly pointing out pennywort growing in a stone wall and opening my eyes to wild food – you have a lot to answer for!

Thank you to Laura Gladwin for believing in me and my writing and all your editing input – four years later here I am! To Tessa David, for your hours of honing my work and tireless effort to get my book into the world; it's here! To Sarah Coetzee, my sister, for your pedantic direction of my grammar, even if I still don't understand semicolons. To Elliott White for your visual eye and being up for this project – here it is, your photography in a complete book.

To Pete, Katrina, Terrie, Amanda and all my friends who cast their eyes over my writing and gave me your feedback. To Erwin, Amanda and Dan for letting me go through your cookery books, for your visual input and helping me imagine where this book sits.

To Mum (again), Corinne, Winnie, Valentine, Tamara, Jonny, Amanda and, of course, Emily Kydd for all your recipe testing and feedback. Emily – you were a joy to work with and so glad you discovered cleaver-seed coffee! To all my friends and family (including Elana and Fin) who've been eating my wild and sweet creations for years: eating dessert alone isn't half as fun as sharing it with you.

Thank you to Kim Walker and Janet Hay for checking my input and accuracy of the plants' potential medicinal benefits – your skills and knowledge remain essential to me and the world. To Susanna, for your faith in me and my vision for this book and for suggesting Cultivator Cornwall who helped fund the photography. Cultivator – you have helped make this book great!

To all the team at Hoxton Mini Press, especially Martin Usborne for phoning me up and saying 'yes' to this project – you don't know how much of a relief that was to me. To Florence Filose for all your editing hard graft and level-headedness: you made it fun, light and easy. To Ann Waldvogel, Anna De Pascale, Daniele Roa, Becca Jones, Fred Huber and Jane Birch for your skills in bringing this book into the world, as well as Here for your design input and for punctuating this book with more colour and life.

Thank you everyone. I'm so happy and excited that you were part of *Wild and Sweet* – I couldn't have done it without you.

Rachel Lambert is an award-winning author, based in West Cornwall, who writes about foraging and cooking. Her second book *Seaweed Foraging in Cornwall and the Isles of Scilly* won a Gourmand World Cookbook Award in 2017, and she has been leading wild food courses since 2007. When she's not teaching people to forage, you'll find her either happily entangled in the local community, immersed in nature or having a sneaky nap.

wildwalks-southwest.co.uk

Elliott White is a food and interiors photographer, whose aim is to make food look so completely delicious it makes you salivate. He lives in Cornwall, but travels all over the country to photograph some of the UK's most beautiful restaurants and hotels and help share their stories. At home, he and his wife spend their time bringing up their two children (and a crazy cockapoo).

elliottwhitephotography.com

Hoxton Mini Press is a small, east London publisher run by a handful of book-mad people and two dogs, Bug and Moose, who hate books but love foraging (mainly for sticks). When we started the company, people told us 'print was dead'; we wanted to prove them wrong. Books are no longer about information but objects in their own right: things to collect and own and inspire.

hoxtonminipress.com

Wild and Sweet
First edition

Published in 2022 by Hoxton Mini Press, London.

Text © Rachel Lambert
Photography © Elliot White*
Edited by Florence Filose
Recipes copy-edited by Jane Birch
Designed in collaboration with Here Design
Additional design by Daniele Roa and Friederike Huber
Recipe testing by Emily Kydd
Production by Anna De Pascale
Image editing by Becca Jones
*Except for the portrait of Rachel on p.271 by Morgan Cartlidge

Thank you to the following organisations for helping to fund the
photography for this book:

ISBN: 978-1-914314-15-5

Printed and bound by FINIDR, Czech Republic

Hoxton Mini Press is an environmentally conscious publisher, committed to offsetting our carbon
footprint. This book is 100% carbon compensated, with offset purchased from Stand For Trees.

For every book you buy from our website, we plant a tree:
www.hoxtonminipress.com